FORBIDDEN TOUCH

THE DUFORT DYNASTY
BOOK TWO

JULIETTE N. BANKS

COPYRIGHT

Author: Juliette N. Banks

Editor: Jen Katemi

Cover design by: Elizabeth Cartwright, EC Editorial

ABOUT THE AUTHOR

Juliette is an indie steamy romance author who has taken the paranormal romance genre by storm with her popular vampire series, The Moretti Blood Brothers. Not all of her sexy and powerful heroes are supernatural—Juliette now has a series of hot, page-turning contemporary romances readers can't get enough of.

Juliette also has a vast background in consumer marketing and previously published with Random House. She lives in New Zealand with Tilly, her Maine Coon kitty.

Juliette N. Banks website:

DEDICATION

Here's to fifty years of life. In July 2022, when this book launches, I will be celebrating a big milestone. Every single year has made me who I am today—a happy author, writing stories that bring joy to people's lives. I am grateful to each one of you who purchased this and any of my books.

And left a review… hint hint!

BOOKS BY JULIETTE N. BANKS

The Dufort Dynasty
Steamy billionaire romance
Sinful Duty
Forbidden Touch
Total Possession

The Moretti Blood Brothers
Steamy paranormal romance

The Vampire Prince
The Vampire Protector
The Vampire Spy
The Vampire's Christmas
The Vampire Assassin
The Vampire Awoken
The Vampire Lover
The Vampire Wolf
The Vampire Warrior

Realm of the Immortals
Steamy paranormal fantasy romance
The Archangel's Heart
The Archangel's Star
The Archangel's Goddess

FORBIDDEN TOUCH

CHAPTER ONE

Fletcher stood at the front of the room in his luxury triplex penthouse and stared out at the hundred or so guests. Behind all the bow ties and cocktail dresses, the lights of Manhattan skyscrapers twinkled brightly.

"To Daniel and Harper," he said, lifting his Waterford crystal glass half full of whiskey, finishing his toast to the newly engaged couple.

The crowd echoed his words, and the music resumed as his eldest brother scooped up his bride-to-be and planted his lips on hers.

This was now a common occurrence since Daniel had arrived back in New York a few weeks ago with the pretty New Zealander. The two lovebirds had met in Hawaii while Daniel was there on business.

Harper giggled, and then the two of them were surrounded by well-wishers. Above her head Daniel mouthed *thanks* to Fletch.

He gave his brother a mock salute and smiled.

Daniel hated all the attention, Harper even more so, but they loved each other. That was clear to everyone around them.

Fletcher liked Harper. She was sassy, strong, and had a huge heart. More importantly, she loved his big brother and didn't let him get away with any of his dominating shit.

Daniel needed someone strong, and he'd most certainly found that someone in Harper.

Whether that dynamic continued into the bedroom, he really didn't want to know, but from the doe eyes he saw from Harper every time she looked at Daniel, he highly doubted it.

Fletcher accepted a fresh glass of whiskey from the waiter and made his way across the room. He'd offered to host the intimate engagement party at his apartment so the two could disappear when they wanted. Plus, he knew how private Daniel was about his personal space, and Harper was still settling in.

Not just to a new home and country, but a billionaire lifestyle.

While most people would roll their eyes at such a thought—and Fletcher had been born with a silver spoon in his mouth—he could still understand how much of a change it was for her.

Now she had a driver, personal security, and staff in her home most days.

Members of the media were desperate to know her so, when Harper refused to give any interviews, they'd done what they did best. Made it up.

Fletcher had completed his master's in communications, and as the director of marketing and PR for Dufort Hotels, he knew the games the media played very well.

He'd sat down with Harper, along with his PR manager, Olivia Miller, to talk his soon-to-be sister-in-law through a handful of options.

In the end, she said she still didn't want to talk to them.

To complicate matters, Harper was a romance author. The media was having a field day with that, but the upside was it gave her books more awareness in the public eye and sales were up, apparently.

That, and the fact she had a movie/TV show being filmed in one of their hotels in Hawaii had made her perfect media fodder.

Fletcher saw an opportunity to leverage the media attention, as did Olivia, but after sharing their thoughts and getting a resounding *no* from the loved-up couple, they had put their thoughts to bed.

Harper had, however, hit it off with Olivia immediately. It didn't surprise him. Olivia was smart, funny and… totally off limits to him.

Fletcher was her boss and a majority shareholder in the Dufort Hotel chain. Plus, there was the pesky company policy about not fornicating with staff.

The Dufort Anti-Fraternization Policy, as it was officially called.

In other words, no shagging the staff.

Something he wanted to do with Olivia very, very much.

The policy was something they'd put in place over a decade ago. Their father, Jonathan Dufort, founder of the multi-billion-dollar Dufort Dynasty, had a poor track record when it came to keeping his cock in his pants—a fact their mother had learned before drinking herself crazy over many years. So, once the boys had really stepped into senior roles in the business, they had encouraged the policy to continue. Many of the board members fully supported it.

In the early years they'd lost dozens of human resource managers who couldn't manage the constant complaints. Now life was different, and laws had changed.

Still, as it turns out, Johnathan Dufort had been a liability.

Which was why, after being dragged into an extortion attempt by a US senator because of their father's philandering ways, Daniel had organized a coup. They stripped Johnathan of the majority of his shares—paying him out—so he now had less control over the business.

Protecting them all. Shareholders included.

Fletcher and Hunter had supported Daniel's decision, and now the three collectively held the majority shares.

The relationship with their father was now tense, but not broken.

"Great speech, Fletch," someone said, clinking glasses with him as he made his way to the kitchen. Fletcher was used to hosting parties, so it had been no big deal to pull it together last minute.

Or so his executive assistant, Scarlet, had said.

"Fletch, man, how are you?" Trevor, a college friend, asked.

"Good. So glad the timing worked out. I know you're a busy man. Dan's happy you could make it." Fletcher slapped him on the shoulder.

Hunter, his younger brother, joined them.

"Trev, are you leaving?" Hunter asked. "We're heading over to *Joy Club* afterwards. Join us?"

Joy Club.

Yeah, it was exactly as it sounded and not at all Fletcher's scene.

Trevor shook his head. "Can't. I have a big presentation tomorrow, so I need to get a few good hours' sleep in."

Trevor was a medical researcher with a focus on infectious diseases. Though he was young, he was making great strides in his career already.

"On a Saturday?" Fletcher asked, even though he was guilty himself of working outside normal business hours.

Dufort had hotels all over the globe including Australia, England, Europe, and the United States, so the varied time zones meant he met with his large marketing team at weird hours.

He was often at networking events which were never painful no matter where or when they were held, because he was always surrounded by gorgeous women. Which was one reason he'd earned the title "Playboy of Manhattan" by the tabloids.

"Hey, *I'm* still working on my first billion, Dufort," Trevor joked. "But yeah, a fucking Saturday."

They all knew Trevor was never going to starve. His whole family was made up of medical professionals and his father was the CEO of the New York Presbyterian—the largest hospital in the country.

"If I said we had a private room booked, would that sway you? It's been years man, come on." Hunter tapped Trevor on the arm with his tumbler.

Fletcher grinned and turned away to leave them to their conversation. There were two years between each of the Dufort brothers and when Daniel had befriended Trevor at Harvard, he'd joined them for some of the holidays. Hunter may have been the youngest, but the two of them had bonded over their common interest in some kinky shit.

Totally not Fletcher's thing.

Not that he was a vanilla lover—not at all. But whips and stuff?

Nope.

Hunter had always been a control freak so he could only imagine—though he tried not to—what his younger brother was like in the bedroom.

Or wherever the guy liked to fuck.

"Next time, Hunt," Trevor replied, slapping him on the shoulder. "Enjoy, but right now I better go say goodbye to Daniel. Harper's lovely, isn't she?"

Both of them nodded.

"She's perfect for him." Fletcher sipped his whiskey as he watched Harper run her hand mindlessly up and down Daniel's chest. She had a dreamy look in her eyes that was mirrored in her fiancé's.

Who would have thought?

A Dufort brother getting married. After what they'd seen their mother put through, all three of them had said a hard no to matrimonial *not-bliss*.

At thirty, Fletcher was in no hurry to even think about settling down.

Like most men in his position, he had a lot of choice when it came to women. He was 'ridiculously good looking with those green eyes and muscled physique', to quote *Forbes*.

The brothers had gotten their looks from their father and God knows the man had put his to good use over the decades.

Buzz buzz.

Fletcher slipped his hand inside his gray Prada jacket and pulled out his phone.

Olivia.

His cock twitched.

God damn it.

New York Daily News *is asking for an exclusive on the launch. Yes? No?*

Fletcher flipped his wrist and glanced at his watch.

Ten damn o'clock.

What the hell was Olivia doing working on the media for the SoHo Dufort launch this late on a Friday night?

Liv, shut down your laptop and have a drink. Or go dancing. NYDN can wait until Monday.

And it could.

The launch of their new luxury hotel in SoHo was another week away, which was an eternity in the media world.

Yeah, yeah, I'm leaving soon. I have a demanding boss.

Fletcher snorted.

Wait.

Was she still at the office?

He pressed call.

"Fletcher," Olivia purred.

Okay, she didn't purr, but in his head she had. Like a damn sex kitten.

He stepped away from the crowd and walked through his penthouse to the private dining area. He left the lights off and stepped up to the floor-to-ceiling glass windows.

Three stories of glass.

"Why are you still in the office? Is anyone else there?" he asked, purring back.

Olivia groaned. Like, actually did.

He squeezed his eyes shut as his cock began to stand to attention.

"I wanted to lock in the media before Monday. Next week is going to be busy, and I get Sammy back on Sunday night."

Sammy was Olivia's six-year-old daughter. A little mini-me. Flaming red hair that curled haphazardly around her head with bright blue eyes. Just like her mom's.

"It'll be fine. You need to start delegating to Katy and Thomas more."

"Not this stuff, you know I can't," she said, and he could tell by her voice she was distracted, packing up. "Anyway, how many bosses ring to tell their employees off for working late?"

The corners of Fletcher's lips curled into a small smile. He put the call on speaker and sent off a text.

"I haven't done a survey, so I can't answer that, but I've just sent Frederick your way, so he will be downstairs in five minutes. He's driving you home." He spoke firmly.

"Fletcher." She replied in a little growl.

He smiled. "Don't argue. I'm your boss."

"I can take the subway just like the rest of New York."

Yeah, no, fuck that.

He hated that Olivia used the subway at all, but it wasn't his place to say anything. But working this late for his company?

No.

That, he got a say in, and he wasn't taking no for an answer. He would make sure she got home safely.

"Don't leave him hanging. You know he hates it," Fletcher said, staring out at the lights with his phone back on his ear and his other hand in his pocket.

He knew right now Olivia would be scrunching her nose and silently mouthing something rebellious.

They had worked closely together for nearly two years, so he knew her pretty well. Although recently Olivia had invaded his thoughts more and more, and he realized he wanted to know a lot more about her.

Despite the damn company policy.

She had a daughter.

He'd hired her so he knew she had extensive media and public relations experience in the hotel and tourism industries.

He knew she was single.

At least, he thought she was single.

He knew she was divorced and shared custody of Sammy with her ex.

Fletcher didn't know how she spent her time outside of work, except for the obvious requirements of being a mom.

She let out another groan. "Thank you. See you Monday."

"Olivia," he said, stopping her.

Fletcher didn't know what he was going to say. He just didn't want to hang up.

There was a long silence before she replied.

"Yes?" she whispered.

Shit. Shit. Shit.

"Have a good weekend," Fletcher replied finally.

CHAPTER TWO

Damn him.

Olivia sat in the back of the black luxury car and hugged her purse against her chest. Her laptop bag sat on the seat next to her as the warm air-conditioning brushed lightly against her skin.

It was certainly much nicer than the subway. She wasn't going to argue with that, but Olivia knew it was inappropriate for her to keep accepting these little things Fletcher did for her.

No one had noticed yet.

As far as she was aware.

And they couldn't.

One wrong move and she could lose Sammy, and there was no way she was going to let that happen.

Three years ago, she had left her husband, Simon, a reporter at *New York Today*. He had been controlling and manipulative for years. She had finally found the strength to ask him to leave, and he had.

After a lot of yelling.

She had been proud of herself as they navigated shared childcare and their separation until one afternoon a few months after Simon had left, her friend Emma—who also worked as a reporter at *New York Today*—had visited. They had all been friends, and Olivia knew it was going to be hard for everyone to adjust.

When she arrived, Emma had dropped her purse on the sofa and a small bag of pills had fallen out. Olivia wasn't into the drug scene, but she knew exactly what she was looking at when she saw the small white pills with smiley faces on them.

Molly.

"Emma," Olivia said, picking the small plastic bag off the floor and waving it at her. "Seriously, Sammy could have gotten into these."

"Shit, sorry," Emma had replied. "They're not mine. One of the girls from work asked me to take them for her. Long story."

Olivia shook her head.

"I didn't think you were into this stuff."

Emma had flushed, and she'd thought it was weird. She had handed the Molly back to her and Emma had tossed it onto the coffee table.

"I should just flush it down the toilet," Emma had said.

"Doesn't your friend want it back?" Olivia asked, knowing vaguely, as much as the next person, drugs weren't cheap. Throwing someone's stash away seemed like a drastic thing to do, but then again, her *long story* comment had felt loaded, so perhaps it was the right thing to do.

Not her problem, she'd decided, so they drank their coffees and Emma had changed the subject to Sammy and how she was coping with all the change.

In hindsight, it was a clever distraction.

A few minutes later Emma's phone had rung, and she'd jumped up mouthing *media emergency* and flown out the door.

The Molly was left lying on the coffee table.

Olivia tucked them away in the medicine cabinet above the sink where Sammy couldn't find or reach them, intending to give them back to Emma the next time she came over. She was walking back to the sofa to text Emma when she felt odd.

Before she could sit down the room began spinning.

Fifteen minutes later Simon had suddenly shown up, busting down the door. Sammy, who had been having an afternoon nap, began crying and clinging to her while Simon shouted about Olivia taking drugs.

She had been so confused.

Initially Olivia thought she'd suddenly come down with a bug.

That's when Child Protective Services arrived.

Through the foggy buzz in her head, she heard Simon tell them he was her ex-husband, and that she had a history of drug use but had never been caught.

A white-collar user, he called her.

Then they'd found the bag full of drugs in the cupboard. Simon had shaken his head and said something about it being the same stuff she'd taken when they were married.

Lies.

All lies.

She had wobbled and screamed, accusing him of lying and setting her up, looking exactly like a druggie, as they packed up Sammy's things and took her.

Took her damn daughter.

It had taken months of legal action and proving she was not—or in the court's minds, no longer was—a drug user, and that she was a good mother, to finally get her three-year-old daughter back.

The longest time in her life.

With no prior convictions of any kind, including drugs, and no proof to support his claim, along with a solid job history, her lawyer had done an amazing job of getting her shared custody.

Simon and Emma had set her up. They had drugged her. It had been the hardest and most heartbreaking time of her life.

She learned Emma had been sleeping with Simon—for how long? She didn't know—and now they were married.

Every second week Olivia had to hand over her daughter to them, the people who had drugged her, and let them play happy families. She didn't trust them for a single minute. She was constantly on alert, not doing anything that could jeopardize her situation.

She didn't date.

She didn't go out and aside from the odd wine at home or when she was at a work event, she hardly drank.

Work—home—mom life.

That was it.

A few months after getting Sammy back, she had started working at Dufort Hotels.

Of course, she had noticed Fletcher Dufort was an extremely good-looking man.

Okay, fine, he was hot.

Seriously hot.

But he was also smart and funny, and she valued this opportunity. A year into the job, she began to notice how close they had gotten. She was, for all intents and purposes, his unspoken second-in-charge, and the go-to person for marketing and PR queries. It wasn't unusual for that to happen, by the nature of her job, but there was something more.

Olivia began to notice the way he would look at her when he thought she wasn't looking.

Then, when she *was* looking.

And she was doing the same to him.

The tension had slowly built and, after two years, it was becoming impossible to ignore. But he was her manager. Fletcher was the director of marketing and PR. The son of the founder of Dufort Hotels and a majority shareholder.

Even if it wasn't for her situation with Simon, neither of them could act on their attraction to one another. Dufort

Hotels had an anti-fraternization policy which forbade employees having sexual relations with one another.

With one of the Dufort brothers?

No.

With playboy Fletcher Dufort?

Oh, hell, no.

As their PR manager, she knew exactly the type of media attention the Duforts' love lives attracted.

Especially Fletcher's.

And especially now that Daniel was engaged and officially off the market. Fletcher and his brother Hunter, the third Dufort brother, had both recently become equal majority shareholders with Daniel, making them extremely desirable to women.

As if their masculine good looks and tall muscular bodies weren't enough.

Media interest in who Fletcher was dating was insatiable and, because he never dated anyone for long—cough, one night, cough—he had earned the nickname "Playboy of Manhattan".

Fletcher didn't love the attention but because he had a more playful personality than Daniel, who hated the media, and his job involved dealing with them, he would smile and wink at the cameras.

Hunter kept his personal life very private and attended company events only when necessary. She had a little insight as to why. The rumors were, his personal life ran a little darker than standard fare.

So, Fletcher Dufort was off limits for Olivia, and she had her own baggage and reasons to keep her eyes off her extremely charming and sexy boss.

Easier said than done, though.

When he stepped into a room in one of his custom-made tailored suits and gave her a wink, her knees went weak, and… no, that was a lie.

Her knees were fine.

It was her panties that had a problem.

Wet.

Even when he kept his winks to himself, and those green eyes met hers from across the boardroom table, Olivia found herself burning from the inside out.

And he knew it.

"Here we go, Ms. Miller," Frederick announced as he pulled up outside her brownstone.

"Thank you," Olivia said. "You have a lovely evening."

She climbed out of the car and hastily raced up the steps. The last thing she needed was Simon finding out she'd been dropped off home, again, by *the fancy car*.

He'd already made a couple of comments about her relationship with Fletcher Dufort.

She unlocked her front door and then closed it, leaning against the back of it, and let out a long sigh.

Bath.

Wine.

Book.

Bed.

Then one more night and Sammy would be home.

In the meantime, she could fantasize about Fletcher Dufort and what could never be, while making good use of her vibrator.

Olivia pushed the closet door closed and picked up the washing basket. As she walked through the kitchen, she turned the oven on low to heat up the casserole she had baked.

It was already seven o'clock and Sammy would be home in the next hour. Simon never gave her an exact time and always made sure their daughter was tired and hungry when he dropped Sammy off. It only hurt their daughter, but was his attempt to make life miserable for Olivia.

Olivia had to ignore it.

It wasn't worth getting into an argument with Simon. It upset Sammy and ruined her night.

Instead, Olivia had worked out not to prepare anything for dinner that could spoil, and to dish it up as soon as Sammy walked in the door.

Then they had cuddles on the couch watching one of her favorite shows. Usually within an hour and a half, her daughter was calmer and ready for bed.

Then Olivia spent the next hour unpacking her bags and getting her school things ready for the next day. After she had searched them for anything her insane father had put in there that could potentially incriminate her.

Was she paranoid?

Possibly.

Did she think Simon was capable of it?

Absolutely.

Knock knock.

Olivia drew in a long breath.

"Hello, sweetheart." She leaned down as Sammy jumped into her arms.

"Mommmm." Sammy sobbed, and Olivia's eyes lifted to glare at Simon.

He shrugged and shoved a folded note into her hand. She pulled Sammy back and took in her tear-stained eyes.

"What baby?" she said, wiping the hair from her daughter's forehead.

"Daddy forgot to get me a costume, so I'll be the only kid without one." Sammy sniffed. "Can you make me one, Mommy? Please?"

Olivia stood and opened the note. Dress as your favorite book character day was on Monday and the note was dated the Tuesday before.

"Put your bags away, Sammy, and wash up for dinner. I'll make you a costume, don't worry." She ran a hand over her hair.

Her daughter's face lit up with a mix of relief and happiness, then she danced off to her bedroom.

Olivia glared at Simon again.

"What?" he said, "Don't give me shit. I only saw the note yesterday."

Olivia shook her head.

"Yesterday? So, you had two days and still decided to leave it for me on a Sunday night?" she ground out. "Seriously, Simon, you're only hurting our daughter with this fucked-up behavior."

His face turned angry.

"Watch your mouth," he snarled, pointing a finger at her. "You're lucky to have her at all."

Olivia rolled her eyes.

"You and I both know you set me up. Now get the hell out of my doorway. I have a costume to put together."

She began to push the door closed, but he didn't budge.

"Simon," she warned, but her heart began to pound.

His eyes ran over her body for a long moment, then, full of anger, they met hers.

Why couldn't he just move on? He had married Emma and hurt Olivia more than anyone ever could. Wasn't that enough?

She was just exhausted by it all.

One day, when their daughter was a legal adult, Olivia would be free of his control. Until then, she had to learn to keep her mouth shut.

He was unstable and dangerous to provoke.

Simon reached out and tucked her hair behind her ear. She felt vomit rise in her throat.

"Watch your back, baby-cakes." He smirked before walking away.

Olivia's legs turned to jelly as she shut the door and slid the bolt. Resting her head on the doorjamb, she counted to ten and then let out a long breath.

"What do you think about Captain Underpants?" she called out, walking into the living room.

"Noooo. Mom!"

Eh, worth a try.

CHAPTER THREE

Fletcher climbed out of the car and pulled his coat tight around him. It was still cold in Manhattan, being early April. Next month, it would start to warm up.

The doorman pulled open one of the large glass doors to the Dufort building.

"Good morning, Mr. Dufort."

"Morning, Douglas."

He looked around the large lobby and considered buying a coffee at the café. It was busy, so he decided to send his secretary down for one.

The escalators were lined with people moving up and down, and to the right, dozens of people waited for one of the elevators.

Fletcher made his way to the left, where the executive elevators gave him private access to their floor.

One of them opened and Daniel stepped out.

"Fletch. I was just coming to see if you'd slept in."

Dick.

It was barely seven thirty.

"No, you weren't," Fletcher replied, laughing, then stepped into the elevator. He pressed his thumb on the scanner to activate it and the doors began to close.

He looked up as Daniel smirked. "See you at SoHo Dufort at ten."

Fletcher nodded.

This was an important launch for Dufort Hotels. While it was their third hotel in Manhattan, it was the first luxury boutique hotel in their portfolio—the flagship.

Over the past month the teams had been preparing for the opening. Daniel's visit, as their CEO, was an important date in the launch calendar.

Daniel wasn't as hands-on as he once had been. Their father had insisted they all learn and understand the entire business from the ground up, while being groomed for their executive positions, so he knew his brother was looking forward to seeing SoHo today. Keeping him away and out of the detail had been a challenge at certain points.

Hunter was the director of sales. He'd always had more of an affinity with the commercial numbers, and so was responsible for getting return business from their guests, negotiating with vendors, overlooking their conference and event spaces and anything that touched the customer experience such as the front of house. Of course, he had a huge team, globally, that did the more hands-on management and tasks.

Fletcher, even from an early age, navigated to all things media and talking to their customers. Marketing was about molding those two things and influencing people to make decisions. Or, in the case of their clients, choosing a Dufort Hotel for their next holiday or business trip.

They had hotels around the world, and with time zones, his global marketing team was constantly working on different promotional campaigns, such as Easter, Valentine's Day, or Christmas.

Or dealing with any number of media requests or crises. From one day to the next they could be answering questions about someone dying in one of their rooms, which happened way more often than most people realized. Or about how sustainable their hotels were, or whether a celebrity was staying with them.

And everything else in between.

Which was where Olivia came in. She was a public relations expert.

Fletcher had hired her two years ago after spending a lot of time choosing the right candidate. Mostly because he knew he would be working with this person very closely.

Olivia had two team members in New York—Katy and Thomas—and a handful of others who looked after key regions in Oceania and Europe.

Fletcher had been impressed with Olivia from the day she started. She had an excellent work ethic, managed her relationships with the media well and had a quick mind, often thinking outside the box when they were in a crisis.

She seemed to enjoy, as much as he did, batting around ideas while the two of them mulled over challenging situations.

Often, they guzzled coffee in his office and used whiteboarding strategies.

Fletcher pulled his laptop out of his bag and plugged it into his docking station, then slipped off his Tom Ford coat.

"Morning Mr. Dufort." Scarlet, his personal assistant, took his coat and hung it up in the wardrobe. "Coffee?"

"Yes, God. A long black please, Scarlet." He needed something strong this morning. "Is Olivia here yet?"

"No, sir." She left to get his elixir.

Fletcher took a moment to catch his breath, gazing out at the view of Manhattan and the field of rooftops. He spotted one or two helicopters landing and taking off, transporting executives like him to their offices, and saw the sun finally peeking through the clouds.

His eyes returned to his office and the sofas where he'd spent hours with Olivia.

Had he found her attractive when they met?

Absolutely.

She was a beautiful woman, even with all her wild red curls. Still, Fletcher was surrounded by gorgeous women, so there had been no red flag warning him not to employ her.

Frankly, they all blended into one another most days.

At the time, he'd been focused more on her experience and impressive interview. He had been confident she would do a great job and be passionate about working for the Dufort brand.

And she had been.

Because he was ultimately responsible for the Dufort name and its reputation, they worked closely every day. He did the same with all his managers, but public relations required more of his attention, as it had with Olivia's predecessor.

Over time they had built a solid professional relationship, getting to know one another a little more personally as any colleagues who worked closely together did.

Until one day things shifted.

First, he noticed her laugh. Like, *really* noticed it. In a different way.

Her eyes had sparkled, and their gazes held as they shared a joke. They had caught themselves and looked away.

One day he found himself taking in the curve of her breasts during a meeting which, thankfully, no one else was in. She had glanced up and his eyes had met hers. Time had slowed as they both acknowledged silently how their connection was shifting.

Fletcher knew, even back then, he needed to do something to control his reaction to her. The last thing he wanted was for Olivia to resign. Or make a complaint.

He tried to mask his feelings.

Then he realized his attraction wasn't one-sided.

During a global marketing meeting, where team members outside of the United States were connected in via video conference, Fletcher had been standing at the front of the room presenting. With multiple cameras and screens set up he had glanced into one of them and caught her staring at him.

Like *that*.

Full of rich heat.

He'd stared into the camera and then slowly swiveled around, and their eyes had locked.

The entire world had vanished in that millisecond as they silently acknowledged the chemistry between them. Thick need and desire flared to life in her eyes and then she had swallowed and dropped her gaze to her tablet.

Fletcher knew in that moment they were in trouble

He had a choice. He could pursue her and breach the Dufort company policy—his own fucking company—that prohibited employees from fraternizing.

Including him.

Or he could... fire her.

And there was no way he was losing a talented employee because he couldn't control his damn cock.

So he'd been *managing* it.

Not his cock.

That was out of control—he'd been jerking off daily and it wasn't helping at all.

Then one night he'd slipped up.

A simple hand on the small of her back as they were leaving a meeting, and Daniel had noticed the connection.

Hell, he hadn't even noticed how they were standing closer, touching more, grinning at each other more.

But they were.

Fletcher didn't want to lose her. She was an excellent PR manager, and he knew she needed this job. She was a single mom and... he cared about her.

He was determined to deal with this.

Perhaps he needed a holiday in Bora Bora with a movie star, or supermodel, or some half-naked blond.

The media hadn't given him that ridiculous nickname for nothing. He had slept with many gorgeous, rich, and famous women. Like his brothers, Fletcher was photographed at events with the latest on his arm and the usual tabloid gossip about whether they were dating, getting married, or about to become parents.

He could have saved them all the trouble.

He would be doing none of those things.

Daniel may have fallen, but Fletcher had no intention of marrying and suffering through a miserable marriage like his parents.

And being a parent? Jesus, no.

It appeared he loved sex as much as Jonathan Dufort. He wasn't going to put a child through the same misery that he'd endured, watching his father disrespect his mother and fuck everything else in sight.

There were seven billion people on the planet. That was a sufficient number to keep his cock busy until he was dead.

Eventually, he'd find someone to take his mind off Olivia. Until then, he'd... well, he hadn't worked out a solution yet.

But he'd find one.

Or a *someone*.

An hour later, a flash of red caught his attention.

"I'm here, I'm here. Sorry, I had a costume emergency," Olivia said as she raced into his office.

Fletcher smirked as he took in her white wool dress and red jacket.

"Are you aiming for a nineteen-fifties nurse? Because I have to tell you, Olivia, you're missing a few details."

She bunched her brows, and then they widened.

"Not me. Sammy!"

He'd known exactly what she meant, but he loved teasing her.

She glanced down at herself. "Do I look like a nurse? Oh, my God. I look like a nurse. Shit. I just grabbed the first clean thing in the wardrobe."

"I was joking. Relax." Fletcher smirked.

Olivia plonked herself in the chair in front of his desk and let out a breath. "You're cruel."

"Coffee?" he asked, and as if by magic Scarlet popped her head in the door.

"Chai latte, please," Olivia ordered.

"Please shut the door," he called out, then turned to Olivia. "Good weekend?"

He tried, and failed, to ignore the curve of her breasts under the hug of her dress, and the red of her plump lips. Then she slightly tugged her bottom lip between her teeth and his pants tightened.

Dammit.

Fletcher cleared his throat and picked up a pen, studying it as if his life depended on it.

"Yes. Thanks for the ride home," she replied, and he looked up into her bright blue eyes. "You?"

"What?"

"Your weekend. Was it good?" Olivia asked.

I got trashed on Friday night because I couldn't stop thinking about wanting to rip your panties off and fuck you on my desk. Then I jerked off all weekend instead of going out with a gorgeous actress.

"Yes," he said instead. "Pretty low key after the engagement party."

"Oh, the party. Did Harper look beautiful?"

Fletcher smiled to himself. The two women got along great. Harper had said he should invite Olivia along, but given Daniel's awareness of his attraction to his PR manager, he had decided against it. Especially given his resilience around her was slipping. Whiskey plus Olivia in a cocktail dress equaled disaster.

"That's a question for my brother." He smirked.

"Show me a photo. Come on," Olivia pressed. "She's so lovely. You must be so thrilled to have such a nice sister-in-law."

Both he and Hunter adored Harper. She was down to earth, funny, and talented in her own right. She had a successful author career and was totally in love with their brother.

Even better, she didn't take his shit.

When they weren't making silly eyes at each other, the two of them were debating over something which usually ended in Harper winning.

They seemed to have it all.

Love, passion, and commitment.

Something he never thought Daniel even wanted, let alone would end up having.

Still, he was happy for them both. Very.

He just knew it wasn't for him.

Hunter had shared his sentiment during the engagement party.

"Good for Dan. Standing beside him when they get married is the closest I'll ever get to being at a wedding party, though," Hunter had said.

"Same, bro. Same," Fletcher had responded.

He pulled out his phone and shook his head. "Fine. Come around here."

Scrolling as Olivia raced around his desk and sat on the edge beside him, he found some images from the engagement party and handed her his phone.

As she *ooed* and *ahhed*, he breathed in her unique personal scent. It was a mix of jasmine and vanilla with a hint of coffee.

"Oh, her dress is gorgeous." She sighed, swiping, then froze. "It's so… oh. You. You look… great."

Fletcher frowned as she stared at the phone for a long minute, then handed it back to him. It was a photo of him leaning against the window, whiskey in hand, as he laughed along with a group of people.

Hunter had taken it and pinged it to him.

Olivia drew in a breath, and he looked up, both of them suddenly realizing how close they were.

They both stood simultaneously, making the situation worse.

Staring down as Olivia's lips parted, he ached to pull her against him.

Olivia's eyes lifted from his broad chest to his eyes.

Fuck.

He wanted to suck on those lips, lift her onto his desk and part her legs. He bet she was wet right now as her body reacted to his.

His fingers moved an inch—

"So," she said, slipping away and returning to her side of the desk. "Did you have a chance to consider the exclusivity with *New York Daily News*?"

Fletcher glanced at the clock just as Scarlet knocked on the door.

"Come in," he said, and she did, handing Olivia her coffee. God, that was close. So fucking close.

"No, I haven't," he said to Olivia, continuing their conversation. "Tell me what you think."

Olivia sipped her drink, as they got down to business as usual.

As if nothing had almost happened.

"I recommend we don't," she said. "No exclusivity. We want mass media coverage on this. It's a flagship launch, so we want international attention and curiosity about where we'll be opening next."

Fletcher nodded.

"We can offer them an exclusive on our next announcement to soften the blow."

He tipped his head from one side to the other. "Why would we?"

"They're owned by the largest network in the United States. We can leverage this for other spots and possibly some web or TV coverage when we're ready," Olivia said. "I'm thinking long term strategy here, not just this one event."

She deserved more than his lustful thoughts, but the truth was he desired her body and her smart mind.
And to prove it, the hard length inside his pants hadn't subsided an inch.

"Good. Go ahead, but be selective in who we invite. Top ten or twenty. I don't want it to be a circus," he replied.

Olivia smiled. "Agreed."

He lifted his wrist and took in the time.

"Are you running late for something?"

No, but the last thing he needed was Daniel walking in with all the sexual tension hanging around. He'd pick up on it immediately.

"Yes, I'm heading to SoHo in a few minutes for Daniel's visit, so I need to get going. Do you need anything more?"

Olivia shook her head, picked up her chai latte and turned to leave. "Shall I arrange for Tracey to join you to take the photos?"

Tracey was the internal communications advisor, focusing on keeping employees around the world up to date with important information and what was happening in all the regions. It was an important role impacting the company culture and keeping engagement high.

He flinched.

Normally he'd invite Olivia to something like that, even though media wasn't attending. It was important; she was across anything that was about to be launched publicly.

Fletcher realized he was keeping her out of the loop because of his attraction to her. And that was unacceptable.

She turned when he didn't respond. "Fletcher, we need to capture this. For press, and internal communications. Daniel is our CEO, and this is his first visit to our flagship boutique hotel."

She frowned at him.

Christ.

He needed to get his act together. From the look on Olivia's face, it was clear she knew he was trying to put space between them—which was true, but he also wanted to be near her every second he could—and she'd just called him out on a simple fuck up.

Next time, it could be more important.

Internally, he groaned.

"You're right. Grab your things. You're coming with me."

CHAPTER FOUR

Olivia slipped her arms into her coat and pulled it over her shoulders as she exited the executive elevator, followed by her boss.

Why did just standing next to Fletcher Dufort feel sexual? It was utterly ridiculous, and yet it still did.

Sure, his six feet two inches towered over her, but he had a powerful and magnetic essence she'd never felt before.

It was in the little things.

When he sat next to her in meetings, she was constantly aware of his solid muscular thighs stretching the material of his pants, or his large hands as they moved when he spoke or lay on the table between them.

It was in the way his square jaw, sprinkled with dark growth, would clench when they were trying to solve a challenge or lips that smirked when he'd tease her.

Or his smoldering green eyes that watched her when he didn't think she knew.

She knew all right. Her entire being was aware of every single move he made.

He was a difficult man to ignore, least of all because he was a large, powerful and rich man. But then again, so were Daniel and Hunter Dufort, and neither of them made her thighs clench.

Fletcher's hand on her back halted her.

His touch burned.

"We need to wait here a moment." He glanced at his phone while they stood by the glass floor-to-ceiling entrance. "Frederick is fighting traffic."

Around them people went this way and that, employees nodding a greeting at the Dufort executive, while some murmured *hello sir*.

His eyes dropped to hers and she tried to ignore the rich green globes she'd seen in her dreams. She cleared her throat, aware they were standing far too close for colleagues and yet neither of them moved.

"It's warming up," she suddenly blurted out. It totally wasn't. It was still pretty chilly.

Fletcher's lips curved then his eyes darted to his phone as it buzzed.

"Let's go." His hand landed in the small of her back again and he guided her outside.

She really wished he wouldn't do that.

"Ms. Miller. Mr. Dufort," Frederick said as he opened the door for them.

They slid into the back of the car, which was warm and entirely too intimate for the two of them to be alone. Olivia pulled off her coat and lay it on her lap. She turned to Fletcher and found him staring out the window, his jaw rigid.

She knew why.

He was beating himself up for touching her. For wanting her.

This is what he did over and over.

Even when a smile went too far between them, moments later, he'd shut down and become grouchy. She wanted to tell him it wasn't just him, but he knew, and yet she could see he blamed himself.

She wanted to tell him it didn't matter, that even without the Dufort policy in place, nothing could ever happen.

Perhaps she should?

This tension between them was getting worse. If she wanted to keep her job, Olivia knew she had to keep things professional.

Not that they hadn't, but their chemistry was only growing stronger every day.

His hand landed on the leather seat between them, and her eyes followed. She felt him turn to her and her eyes snapped to his.

Shit.

He drew in a deep breath.

It was wrong, but Olivia had fantasized about these moments in the car with him when he'd slide his hand between her legs, feeling her hot and wet for him.

It would take a simple decision.

Or simply act.

And it would destroy everything.

She could lose her job and lose Sammy.

Despite her desire to be touched by this gorgeous man, she would be a fool to let it happen. Fletcher was known as a playboy for a reason. While working for him she'd fielded hundreds of calls from media asking who was the latest woman on his arm at social events.

Her team never responded, of course, and Fletcher never gave them any details of his personal life. They were simply to smile and say no comment.

So they did.

To all of them.

If Olivia was to give in to this powerful attraction between them, she knew she'd end up being just another name on his list.

If he had a list.

Probably not.

The point was, she had no desire to be one of those women. She loved her job and enjoyed working with Fletcher. She actually liked him as a person. As a man.

Perhaps he would meet someone serious and whatever this was between them would fizzle out. Perhaps he already had? There had been no photos of him in the tabloids for the last several weeks.

He'd had a minor surgery, which could be the reason.

Or he could have a girlfriend.

Olivia pressed the button on the side of the phone and her screen lit up with a photo of Sammy. She just had to stay focused on keeping her daughter safe and with her.

That was her priority.

Fletcher shifted beside her. She moved her coat and found her dress had crept up. He cursed quietly, and her eyes snapped to his. They were dark and full of hunger.

Shit, shit, shit.

"Is there a schedule for today's tour or are we in the hands of the hotel manager?" she spat out in desperation to keep things focused.

Fletcher ran a hand over his face and through his hair, mussing it up. God, he looked so damn sexy.

Is that what he'd look like laying over her?

She chewed her bottom lip just as his eyes found hers again.

Oh crap.

"Liv," Fletcher said thickly.

Her lips parted as heat flushed through her body and she realized, in the moment he spoke her name, their world changed.

She couldn't. She couldn't let this happen.

There was too much at stake.

"Please... we can't." Olivia said, squeezing her eyes closed momentarily. When she opened them again, Fletcher reached out slowly and threaded his fingers into her hair.

She let him.

Or at least she didn't stop him.

Her entire being wanted him to touch her. She burned for him.

"This is getting really fucking hard," Fletcher said, cupping the side of her face.

His words had no context if you were an observer. Neither of them had spoken of their desire for one another.

But she knew exactly what he meant.

They both did.

She nodded, her mouth dry. "I know."

His eyes roamed over hers and down to her lips. The temptation to lean in and change both their lives even more was a breath away. The hunger in his eyes surely matched hers, and when she unconsciously licked her lips, Fletcher's arm suddenly dropped.

"Shit," he cursed, as both relief and disappointment laced through her body. "I shouldn't have done that."

Olivia stared at the seat in front of her. Her body burned with need and her heart thumped anxiously.

God, what had they done?

"At least we've acknowledged it. This. Now we have to find a way to stop it," she said.

The car pulled up outside SoHo Dufort and Fletcher shot her a look rich with the promise that this wasn't over.

Not at all.

Olivia walked around the lobby of the new hotel, admiring the décor and luxurious touches that were unique to this new brand. It would attract the wealthy corporate traveler, and they'd accommodated everything a busy executive would need.

Every inch of the space was high quality and screamed expensive, from the large chandeliers to the black and gold carpets and custom-made furniture.

Olivia had visited the site during construction, so it was fantastic to finally see it complete.

Mostly, she was trying to keep her distance while Fletcher spoke to the manager and staff. Even with her back to him, she could feel his eyes on her.

The worst part was she wanted to be the center of his attention.

Hell, what woman wouldn't?

Fletcher Dufort was drop dead gorgeous. He was the full package. Successful, wealthy, charming, funny, and he had the most kissable lips she'd ever set eyes on.

Olivia turned and took in his tall, powerful body. Even beneath his expensive tailored suit, his muscles were impossible to disguise. And she was very familiar with his strong forearms after watching him roll up his shirt sleeves in countless meetings.

"Good morning, everyone," Daniel said as he stepped into the lobby, looking every bit a powerful CEO, and shaking everyone's hands. "Olivia."

"Morning, sir." She smiled.

"Right," Fletcher said. "Hunter isn't here yet, but let's get moving, so we stay on schedule. Aaron is going to lead the tour, so over to you."

"Is there anything you want to see first, sir?" Aaron, the hotel manager, asked.

Daniel shook his head just as Hunter arrived.

"Hey. Sorry. Late," the younger Dufort brother said, and she grinned.

He was kind of lovable.

Fletcher shot her a look, and she smiled privately to herself.

"About time," Daniel said. "Olivia—"

"She's taking photos. For staff and the media," Fletcher said, and they all stared at him.

"Thanks, Einstein. I worked that out all on my own." Daniel narrowed his eyes, then turned to her. "I was going to say I want you to ensure no one from the media asks about our upcoming nuptials."

Fletcher glanced away and she could see he was kicking himself for his reaction. He had always been a touch protective of her but now things were getting a little irrational.

And Daniel was a very sharp and intelligent man.

If he hadn't already, he would work this out.

Then she'd be out of a job.

"I can do my best, but as you know, we can't control what they ask, unless it's paid media. And this isn't," she replied.

Daniel nodded at her knowingly. "Just use your magic powers."

Olivia laughed. "Okay."

The inside joke calmed her. She was often complimented on the way she dealt with the media and got them to do the company's bidding.

It wasn't easy—her relationships with members of the media had been built over years and often she achieved results by negotiating and haggling.

Basically, it was like juggling promises and calling in favors.

And yes, she had a spreadsheet.

Over the next two hours, they wandered through the hotel, admiring the rooms and little touches they all knew the media would focus on. She took photos of the three Dufort brothers with Aaron and then a few of Daniel, so the teams had a bunch to choose from.

She excused herself early so she could escape another intimate moment with Fletcher in the car, and his short nod told her he was well aware that was what she was doing.

Back at the office, she was flicking through the photos when her team filed through the door.

"Are we having our team meeting?" Katy asked.

"Yes. Grab a seat," she replied, waving at both Katy and Thomas, directing them to the meeting table in her office.

She joined them.

"Have you signed off on the press release I sent?" Thomas asked.

"I've just sent it to your inbox, with some minor changes," Olivia replied. "Katy, you can please work with the design team in the photos. I'm going to email you. Once both those are done, we should be on track to send the media kit out in time for the launch this Friday."

"Do you want us to follow up on RSVP's?" Katy asked.

Olivia pursed her lips in consideration.

"Good question," she replied. "This is a VIP event, and if they've forgotten about us, then we've failed. Resending it feels desperate."

Katy tapped her pen on her lips. "And if we've failed?"

Olivia smiled.

Katy was a little firecracker and was learning fast. The thing about media relations was much of it was using your instincts, and while there was a strategy to it, you could never be sure where people's loyalty was from day to day.

So you had to stay in reactive mode, and not play your cards too soon.

"Then we're in trouble." She laughed, then pursed her lips. "I tell you what. Why don't you two hit Frame Bar on Wednesday night? Take the corporate credit card—but don't go crazy—and see what you overhear."

Frame Bar was the hot spot for NYC reporters during the week. Unless there was a story breaking, many of them were there rubbing shoulders with each other, networking.

"Undercover PR. I like it." Thomas grinned.

Katy laughed and jumped up to get the card from Olivia's desk. "Can we drop into the new hotel and have a look around beforehand so we can legitimately rave about how awesome it is?"

Olivia waved her hand. "Of course, sorry, I should have invited you today, but it was last minute. Ring Aaron's secretary and arrange a time to go down. Here's a few snapshots."

She slid her phone across the table and the three of them began looking through the photos she had taken.

"What's up with Fletcher?" Thomas asked, narrowing his eyes. Olivia frowned and moved to glance at the photo he was referring to. "He looks... mad or something."

Fletcher wasn't angry. He was staring at her as she took the photo, tortured with need.

Just as she was.

This was bad. Really bad.

"Let's choose one with just Daniel."

A few hours later, Olivia slid her bag onto her shoulder and turned to leave her office when she found Fletcher standing in the doorway.

She froze beside her desk.

"Hey."

"Can we talk?"

"Of course," she said as he stepped in and closed the door behind him.

"I wanted to apologize for this morning. It completely goes against company policy and was inappropriate of me." He plunged his hands into his pockets.

His jacket was gone, and his white shirt was rolled up those muscular forearms. On his wrist the large silver watch he wore most days snagged on the material of his pants and his tie was slightly loosened showing an inch or two of naturally tanned smooth skin.

Not that she should be noticing those things.

Olivia averted her gaze, trying to pretend he was just any other colleague.

She failed.

"Fletcher. You don't need—"

"I do. I don't want you to feel uncomfortable at work, Olivia," Fletcher said.

Olivia. Not Liv.

She frowned.

He was right to apologize. For an employee to breach the policy was one thing, but one of the owners was quite another.

But they both knew this wasn't him taking advantage of her because of his position of power. Both of them had given little hints of interest over the past few months and allowed their chemistry to fester.

"I don't," she said, meeting his eyes. "This isn't one-sided. You know that, right?"

The air between them turned electric, the few feet between them felt a mile wide, demanding they close the gap. As much as she wanted his touch, she couldn't let them cross the line.

Sammy was too important.

"I need you to know I haven't done this before. With anyone," he said.

Olivia's lips stretched into a smile, and he let out a laugh.

"You know what I mean. With an employee. Obviously."

"Obviously. And nothing really happened."

"You know that's not true."

"Fletcher, we all know the stories about your father but you're nothing like that. This is not like that."

"That may be true. But Olivia, I need you to know—if you don't already—I want you." His eyes held hers and the fire burning between them notched up to full-on blazing.

Shit.

"God damn it." He took a step forward then halted as if he was forcing himself. "I want to fuck you so damn much, and I don't know how to stop wanting it."

Her lips parted, and her pussy flooded with moisture. She wanted his hands on her. She wanted his mouth on her.

Neither was possible.

Holy hell.

"That's not helping." She groaned, and he took another few steps closer, so she had to tilt her head. "Oh, God."

They stood barely breathing, his eyes running over her face, her lips, then darkening as they returned to nearly challenge her.

"Go," he ordered, his voice thick with gravel. "Before I do something we can't undo."

She scooted around him and ran out the door.

CHAPTER FIVE

Fletcher stood in the shower, his palm on the wall as the water from five shower heads blasted at him. His hand stroked his cock vigorously, trying to work out his frustration.

For the seventh or eighth time this week.

Since Monday, both he and Olivia had been trying to avoid each other as much as possible, but it was impossible. The nature of their jobs meant they worked closely together. However, Olivia had delegated many of her tasks and even when he personally requested her, she would send Thomas or Katy instead, which infuriated him.

Even though he knew it was the smart thing to do.

He closed his eyes against the harsh spray and imagined her bright red hair beneath his hand as her mouth surrounded his cock. He saw those blue eyes of hers as his cock swelled in his hand and imagined gripping her face and fucking her deep throat as she gagged, bringing him the desperate release he needed.

Fuck.

What Fletcher really wanted was to lay Olivia out on his bed and gaze upon her gorgeous body. He wanted to take his time and touch her, taste her, and completely devour her.

He wanted to cover her body with his larger one and dominate her, filling her, so she screamed his name as he thrust balls deep over and fucking over.

"God's sake." He groaned, gripping his cock again.

He could never do any of those things with her. Never. If he did, he would lose her.

But what if they did?

Too many times this week, Fletcher had considered proposing they get it out of their system.

Just once.

One hot and fucking incredible night.

Surely it would relieve the powerful chemistry between them and stop the torture.

The thing was, Fletcher wasn't sure it would.

Recently, his attraction to Olivia had become so intense his interest in being with anyone else had vanished.

Like fucking zilch.

If he hadn't been so sexually ramped up about her, he would have been booking a doctor's appointment.

Fletcher knew it couldn't go on.

Olivia was the one woman he couldn't have.

Reluctantly, he'd scrolled through his phone and chosen someone to take to the SoHo Dufort launch tonight. Women were eager to slip inside his bed and bank account, so he wasn't lacking options.

The last thing he needed was to be topped up with alcohol and be in the same room as Olivia.

Dakota Smithers was a socialite he'd taken to a few events in past years. She knew he'd ensure she had a good time, and then bid her farewell after their night ended.

It was for that reason he'd selected her.

He dressed in his black tux, ran his fingers through his dark locks, and slipped his feet into a pair of Prada's. Tucking his phone into his jacket pocket, he took one last look in the mirror.

"Don't be your fucking father. Olivia deserves better than you wanting to shove your cock inside her."

Good pep talk.

Downstairs, he climbed into the car.

"Evening, sir. Are we still picking up Ms. Dakota?" Frederick asked.

"Yes. The plan remains the same." He frowned, wondering why the man had even asked. While he wished it was Olivia on his arm, he knew Dakota would be a good distraction.

She wasn't a woman you could ignore.

Proving his point, ten minutes later, Frederick opened the door and Dakota stepped in wearing a stunning silver dress with a low neckline showing off her ample breasts.

Exactly what he needed.

"Hey gorgeous," Dakota said, sliding next to him and planting a kiss on his cheek.

"Thank you for coming," Fletcher said, kissing her on the side of her lips.

"I'm excited to see the new hotel," she replied. "You Duforts always put on a grand event."

She chatted away easily until they prepared to exit the vehicle. Both of them put on their game faces. As soon as they stepped out, the paparazzi camera flashes blinded him.

Dakota slid her hand around his upper arm and posed like a professional. He led her inside where their jackets were taken, and they were handed a glass of champagne. One sip told him it was Krug Vintage.

"Oh, it's stunning," Dakota sighed.

Fletcher smiled.

The place looked different at night. The three large chandeliers were lit up, sending sparkles around the spacious lobby, which was filled with guests.

The champagne was flowing while a pianist played, and another sang dulcet tunes.

The event was black tie so there was a sea of black tuxes while the women filled the room with colorful cocktail dresses, expensive jewelry, and perfumes. Not to be outdone on the jewelry front, Fletcher had no doubt the collective value of the men's watches could put a healthy dent in the national debt.

He led Dakota over to his brothers and introduced her to Harper.

"Nice to meet you. Your dress is gorgeous," Harper said, despite her own being absolutely stunning. The Kiwi was so unaware of her own beauty. He knew that fact was a big part of the reason his brother had fallen in love with her.

New York was a tough city and so were many of the women who populated the wealthy circles the Duforts did. It was another reason he'd invited Dakota. She was less of a bitch than most and would treat Harper with respect. Mainly because she was half promised to a member of the English royal family, so her future was set out for her.

Not that anyone knew that but him.

After sleeping with her the second time, he'd wanted to make it clear this was not leading to anything serious or romantic. She had burst into laughter and reminded him that her father was a billionaire—which he knew—and that she had no interest in his Dufort fortune.

When he'd shrugged and said many of the women he slept with had rich trust funds and still wanted to marry him, she had told him her secret. The promise of a tiara and title was apparently very appealing, though she wouldn't say which royal.

"Good move," Daniel said quietly.

"I'm sorry?" He frowned.

"I was getting worried."

"About?"

"A certain PR manager," Daniel said, slapping him on the shoulder. "I really didn't want to fire you."

Fucker.

As if he could.

"Good luck with that," Fletcher laughed, fighting to conceal his irritation. Not because of the threat—Fletcher, Hunter and Daniel were all equal shareholders in the Dufort Dynasty.

Daniel may be the CEO, but unless he pulled off another coup, he was in no way able to exit Fletcher or their younger brother.

Unfortunately, he had hit a nerve, and Fletcher found himself unable to stop from reacting. "Leave it alone, Daniel. Nothing is going on."

His eyes darkened as he challenged his brother.

Daniel narrowed his eyes. "Jesus. You like her."

"She is an excellent PR manager. Now let it go." He turned to Dakota. "Let me show you around."

CHAPTER SIX

Olivia didn't care.

She shouldn't care.

But she did.

Fletcher was here with Dakota Smithers. He'd taken her to a few events over the past twelve months and the media had run story after story on them, claiming there was a serious relationship. Dakota was a wealthy socialite rumored to be connected to all number of powerful men, including those on other continents.

And she was incredibly beautiful.

So was Fletcher. Not a common word used to describe a man, but he was.

Beautiful. Sexy. Powerful.

His tuxedo fit over his large build like it was made for him. Because it was, and likely cost more than six months' rent in NYC. His hair was slightly curled on the ends, his lips upturned in their cheeky way, as they always were. He stood confidently, taking in his surroundings, those stunning green eyes not missing anything, his hand tucked into his pants pocket, showing a hint of the Rolex watch on his wrist.

Wealthy. Influential. Playboy.

They were all words that described Fletcher Dufort. The man she worked with, and desired.

Olivia sighed.

Tonight, though, she had another distraction.

Simon and Emma were attending on behalf of *New York Today*. She had known it was a possibility and there had been no way to control who was sent when they extended the invitation.

NYDN was a major media outlet and excluding them would have been career suicide. The Duforts needed to reach the millions of followers and readers they had.

So, Murphy's Law, they were both here. Olivia knew Simon would watch her like a hawk tonight.

Since the day she started working for Dufort, he had made snide comments about her relationship with Fletcher. At first, she'd been offended that he would accuse her of sleeping with her boss. Now, the idea wasn't quite as preposterous after all.

Not because Fletcher was the *Playboy of Manhattan*, but because they had genuine chemistry.

At least Olivia liked to think of it like that.

After Fletcher had told her how he felt on Monday she'd been unable to think clearly. It was like her hormones had taken control of her brain. Despite her efforts to keep away from him, it hadn't dampened her feelings for him at all.

The circumstances couldn't be worse. She had to focus and keep away from him or Simon would see what was going on and God only knew what he would do.

Her team was here with her, so she would manage from a distance. Katy had been more than eager to work closely with Fletcher during the week and gain more experience. He had been less pleased and sent Olivia a handful of grumpy emails.

He knew what she was doing, but he didn't understand why or how serious the stakes were for her.

It wasn't *just* the Dufort Hotel Anti-Fraternization Policy. That was part of it, but not everything. Her career was important to her, but keeping her job meant keeping her daughter.

The two things went hand in hand.

If she lost her job, it could give Simon reason to contact Child Protective Services and she would risk losing Sammy once again.

She knew he'd stop at nothing to take her daughter and gain full custody one more time. Because he told her so constantly.

Every day, she ensured she did nothing that could give him ammunition. She barely drank or socialized, worked hard, and on those days she didn't have her daughter, she worked late.

It wasn't much of a life, but it was better than one without Sammy.

Now, life was testing her.

This attraction between her and Fletcher had been building in intensity. Being near him was difficult. Keeping away from him was even harder.

Olivia felt Fletcher's eyes on her.

Their eyes locked, and it was like an electrical storm. Invisible sparks flew everywhere.

Shit.

Olivia looked away and found Simon staring at her. No, he wasn't staring; he was glaring. His jaw worked as fury poured from his eyes.

Fuck.

She frowned and turned away.

How dare he look at her like that?

Fletcher was her boss. She had every right to be watching him or talking to him while she was working.

Something snapped inside her, and Olivia decided to stop this insanity. In normal circumstances, she would be over with Fletcher, finding out what he needed and working the room.

She walked across the room to say hello.

It was insane that Simon thought something was going on. Not only was Fletcher Dufort her employer, but he was also well above her social status, so this entire thing was ridiculous.

She was working. She had a job to do.

Be normal.

"Good evening," Olivia said, all casual and friendly.

"Olivia," Fletcher said in greeting, his eyes darting to Dakota, who gave Olivia a small smile of acknowledgment. They had met at a previous event. Clearly, she was of little interest as the woman immediately turned to chat to the person next to her.

"The place looks great. *New York Post* and NYDN are looking for some photos once Hunter arrives," Olivia said, looking down at her phone as if referencing notes, which she wasn't. "So I'll send Katy over when he gets here."

Out of the corner of her eye, she spotted Emma and Simon moving closer. Emma had a professional long lens camera in her hands, as many of the media photographers did, and it was pointing in their direction.

Olivia quickly turned away, grimacing before she could stop herself.

"What's going on?" Fletcher growled quietly.

"Nothing." She replied quickly and took a step away. "I'll—"

"Olivia." He reached discreetly for her elbow, but there was no such thing as discretion when you were watched like an eagle by those looking for proof to destroy you.

Her eyes shot to his. "Don't," she warned.

Fuck.

She had to get away.

Fletcher's hand dropped and his eyes moved around the room like a tiger seeking its prey.

"Excuse me," she said, putting on a professional fake smile. "I need to use the bathroom."

Before he could reply, she walked away.

Olivia dried her hands on the plush hand towel and threw it in the basket provided. She glanced in the mirror and pressed the clips holding her unruly red curls in place.

She reached into her purse and added some red lip gloss, then took a deep breath.

She'd done nothing wrong.

All she'd done was walk over to her boss and talk business. They'd barely seen each other for days.

She was being paranoid.

Emma and Simon were simply doing their jobs. In all likelihood they were just trying to get a photo of Dakota and Fletcher together. Not her.

She was overreacting.

Typing a quick text to the babysitter, she relaxed when the reply came through a few seconds later to say Sammy had just fallen asleep.

Olivia closed her purse and stepped out into the hallway.

"Hello, Olivia."

The hair lifted on the back of her neck as she came face to face with Simon. He leaned against the wall with his arms crossed, his eyes running over her body from the ground up before meeting hers.

"Nice dress. Someone is hoping to get lucky tonight." He laughed, pressing away from the wall.

"What do you want?" She pushed past him, but he caught her arm.

She turned, glaring at him.

"I don't like the way your boss looks at you, Olivia. What's going on between you two?"

She frowned at him. "What are you talking about? Like you just said, Mr. Dufort is my *boss*."

He let out a little angry laugh.

"Oh, Liv, Liv, Liv. You think I'm that stupid? He's a man. I recognize the hunger in his eyes. You've been sucking his cock, haven't you?"

Ugh. He was revolting.

"Fuck off Simon. We work together. He doesn't look at me in *any* way. You're paranoid."

He let go of her arm.

"If I find out he's been near our daughter, you will be hearing from my attorney." He growled, plunging his hands into his pockets.

Olivia shook her head and turned to face him front on.

"I'm allowed to date, Simon. You're the one living with the drug user and we both know it."

"Watch your mouth." He sneered, leaning closer.

A chill ran down her spine.

Simon had been physical with her when they were together, and she knew better than to provoke him.

She needed to stop talking and walk away.

For Sammy's sake.

"If I get even a sniff my instincts are right and I find out you're fucking Dufort, Sammy will be coming to live with me. Full-time."

Olivia turned and walked away. It was good to be the better person.

Until she wasn't.

She lifted her middle finger into the air without looking back.

"Bitch." He spit the word out as she turned the corner and rejoined the party.

God damn it.

What was she thinking?

She was going to pay for that.

CHAPTER SEVEN

"Hey," Hunter said as he walked up. Fletcher glanced at the glass his brother held. It was a darker liquid than his.

Whiskey.

"You're here. Where did you get that?" Fletcher glanced between his flute and the tumbler in his brother's hand.

"Starbucks."

"Ha fucking ha." Fletcher tried to stop his grin.

Hunter was a smartass, and it was no good to encourage him.

"Place looks good," Hunter said, his eyes darting around. "Is Dad coming tonight?"

Things were tense between the Dufort brothers and their father after they'd all but removed him from the organization, but he'd be there. Johnathan had made a point of attending every single event and meeting he could.

And fair enough.

It had been his business and he'd built it from the ground up. None of them thought he would walk away peacefully.

He was a Dufort.

"Yes, but he's not here yet. Or at least I haven't seen him," Fletcher replied.

He glanced across the room and saw that Olivia had returned. She was with her team and a handful of media answering questions. When she spotted Hunter, he watched her grab Katy and direct her over toward them.

Another obvious attempt to avoid him.

Had he completely destroyed their working relationship?

He knew she felt the same as him—she'd said so. He hated the distance between them, and he hated that her eyes weren't on him. Surely, they could deal with this in another way instead of avoiding one another.

The way she had reacted earlier had been odd.

Something wasn't right.

"Hello, Hunter," Dakota said, tilting her face to accept the kiss he hadn't yet offered.

"Dakota, lovely to see you." Hunter leaned in and did as he'd been silently ordered, kissing Dakota's cheek. Because they were all standing so close, he could only imagine what it looked like from behind.

Click, click, flash, click went the cameras.

Jesus.

"Well, now they'll be saying we're having a menage." Dakota winked at them naughtily while Hunter's eyes darkened as he stared down at her.

Fletcher had always suspected his brother had a thing for Dakota.

"That can be arranged," Hunter replied, then glanced at Fletcher. "Though not with my brother, thanks."

"Feeling's mutual." He shrugged.

"Shame," Dakota said, pouting. "Excuse me, gentlemen, I have to powder my nose and it looks like you are about to be interviewed. Again."

As they watched her walk away, Katy joined them with several unfamiliar faces. She introduced everyone and directed the reporters on who could ask their questions first.

A few minutes into the interviews, Fletcher glanced over Katy's head to see Olivia watching. Their eyes met momentarily, and she quickly glanced away.

Fucking hell.

He wanted to storm over there and shake her, but as he continued to observe her, he noticed something new. Something he'd not seen before.

Fear.

He'd been right earlier; something was spooking her.

"Fletcher, can we get a couple of pictures of the three of you, and a quote from Daniel?" Murray from the *New York Times* asked.

As if on cue, Thomas arrived with Daniel. He nodded to his brother, knowing he was well briefed and prepared.

"Good evening, everyone. Thank you for coming." Daniel stood beside Hunter and tucked one of his hands into his pocket, seeming completely at ease and confident in who he was and what he did.

Because he was.

"We're very excited to be celebrating the opening of our first luxury Dufort boutique hotel, SoHo Dufort, this evening."

Cameras clicked and phones lifted to record the prominent CEO's words.

"SoHo Dufort is a destination hotel for corporate travelers visiting Manhattan and will act as the flagship for any upcoming locations around the world."

Daniel glanced at Fletcher, giving him the floor.

"The top-notch technology in our luxury suites, the executive business center and key locations around SoHo Dufort provides everything a busy corporate traveler needs," Fletcher said. "Without compromising on the luxurious experience that guests at our Dufort properties have come to expect and enjoy around the world."

A younger reporter pushed his phone closer.

"Where can we expect the next Dufort boutique hotel to pop up?"

Bingo.

The billion-dollar question they knew would be asked. Probably for months to come.

Anticipation was gold.

"We'll be announcing that in the coming months. It's a 'watch this space'," Hunter replied, as rehearsed.

Hunter wasn't a fan of the spotlight, preferring to leave those things to Fletcher and Daniel, but for this key event it was important all three of them were visible and united.

His younger brother wouldn't stay long. They all knew it.

"Can we ask about your upcoming nuptials, Mr. Dufort?" one reported asked Daniel.

"You can ask, but tonight is about SoHo," Daniel replied with a brief smile. "When my fiancée is ready to speak publicly, we will look to select someone for an exclusive interview."

Daniel's response, prepared for when the question inevitably popped up despite the media being briefed *not* to ask it, garnered the response they had expected.

Like savage dogs, they clamored to be the chosen one.

Fletcher glanced at Katy, who looked overwhelmed. He gave her a little wink, and she relaxed, smiling gratefully back at him. His gaze ventured further, and he spotted Olivia moving in fast.

"Okay, let's wrap this up," Olivia said, and the media immediately reacted, following her as she led them away.

Katy joined them and answered follow-up questions as she walked. Fletcher was impressed with how Katy had handled everything and intended to let her know.

Daniel turned to him. "All good?"

"They want photos, so if Harper is happy to be in a few, I recommend go ahead and do them. It will keep them happy and off your back for a little while longer."

"I'll speak to her." Daniel nodded and went to join his fiancée. To his left, Hunter tipped his whiskey to his lips and looked around the room.

"One hour and you can leave," Fletcher said, answering his brother's unspoken question.

Hunter was his polar opposite. While he'd happily mingle and network all evening, his younger brother was broody and more of a one-on-one kind of guy.

"Gotcha," Hunter replied, then asked, "Whiskey?"

"Yes, as long as it's not from Starbucks." Fletcher smirked, then his eyes wandered away, looking for a flash of red hair.

"Fletch?" Hunter said, a tone in his voice catching Fletcher's attention.

"What?"

Hunter looked across the room at Olivia. Fletcher's stomach tightened.

"You need to be careful, buddy," his brother said. "You may think you're being discreet, but you're not."

Fuck.

"Nothing's going on," he ground out.

"Don't lie to me." Hunter's eyes darted to his. "Even if you haven't fucked her, you want to and all it would take is someone to watch you both for a few minutes to see that."

Fletcher let out a long breath and cursed.

"Daniel suspects," he admitted.

Hunter nodded. "You'll fuck up her career and your relationship with Dan. You know how he feels about the anti-fraternization policy. Especially after the blackmail attempt. All because of our philandering father and a former employee."

Fletcher's face turned dark. "That's not what this is."

Hunter's brows rose. "Are you in love with her?"

What?

No.

Fuck.

He needed to end this conversation.

"Look, I get it. Message received. Now fuck off and get my whiskey."

Hunter shook his head and placed his empty glass on the table near them. He opened his mouth to say something else, but they were interrupted.

"Hunter Dufort, I've been wondering if you would turn up tonight." A sexy brunette sidled up to them.

Suddenly his brother's expression changed. His eyes darkened and he gave the woman a seductive grin before leading her over to the bar. Fletcher didn't bother wondering if she was someone serious. Hunter was secretive and rarely shared anything about his love life, but he knew his brother wasn't looking for a wife.

Hunter was into darker—or perhaps the word was rougher—sexual experiences than Fletcher and Daniel. He'd never dug for details, and knew he was unlikely to receive any, even if he did ask.

Daniel had once asked Fletcher if they should be worried about Hunter, and he'd shrugged. "As long as it's not illegal, and consensual, then the way I see it is its none of our business. He just has… unique tastes."

And that had been that.

Fletcher watched Olivia making small talk with a group of people; nodding, laughing, taking notes on her phone. His eyes roamed over her figure, taking in the figure-hugging red material that split up the side and dipped in a deep cowl neck.

The dress was sexy as hell, and she looked completely fuckable. If she was trying not to be noticed by him, she had worn the wrong outfit.

She lifted her glass, took a sip, then licked her lips.

Fucking hell.

He slipped his finger under his collar and tugged. There was no way he was spending the rest of the night staring across the room like a teenage boy crushing on a girl. After a week of barely seeing her or speaking to her, Fletcher wanted answers.

What was she scared of?

Like a tiger after his prey, he made his way across the room. When she spotted him coming toward her, her eyes widened and she swallowed.

God, what he'd give to see her do that on her knees in front of him.

He felt like letting out a physical growl.

"Mr. Dufort," Olivia said sweetly, as he stopped beside her. Her eyes swept the group of people around her as if making sure they had heard her impersonal greeting.

He nodded to them with little warmth, and they naturally turned away as he'd intended.

"Olivia," Fletcher replied. "Your team has done a great job this evening."

"Thank you, sir."

Sir?

Fucking hell. She could call him sir as she screamed his name.

"Can I get your assistance with something important, please?" he asked, cupping her elbow and trying to lead her away. She didn't budge. Nervousness filled her eyes as his gaze narrowed. "Now."

"Of course." She nodded and removed her arm from his hold before following him at a distance through the room.

Fletcher's jaw stiffened. A week ago, they would have walked beside each other laughing or talking business. He hated that he had destroyed their relationship.

But it didn't change the desire he had for her.

He led them along a corridor where several conference and meeting rooms sat empty. Opening the door to one of the empty rooms, he indicated for her to enter.

She hesitated.

He raised a brow.

She sighed and walked in, their bodies brushing as she did.

He followed and shut the door.

"What's going on, Olivia?" he asked, the only light in the room trickling in from the city lights outside.

She turned to face him, her body a temptation his fingers were itching to touch. His eyes slid across her neck, down her decolletage to the red dress which gloved her body.

"I'm putting distance between us while we work out how to resolve this… tension."

"And how's that working out?" he asked, taking a step closer. "Because it's only making me want you more."

"Fletch." Her breathing was shallow as she placed her hand on his chest, her fingers curling.

His hand covered hers and he pulled her against him. Every part of him knew this was wrong, and yet here he was.

Her body trembled as his eyes locked with hers.

"You look scared. Why?"

She shook her head.

"Are you scared of me?"

"No."

"Does my desire scare you?"

"No." Her voice was almost a whisper. Desire poured from her eyes.

His cock swelled.

"I can't watch you across the room another minute in this fucking hot dress and pretend it's not affecting me."

She sucked in a breath and her lips parted.

Jesus, he wanted his mouth on hers. He needed to taste her.

"I'm losing this battle, Liv. Tell me I'm not alone."

"I…" she began, then stopped.

"Tell me," he ordered.

Blue moist eyes, burning with desire, met his with such intensity it nearly bowled him over. They said more than her words, but he needed them anyway.

He had to know.

"If you don't want this, I want you to walk out of here right now." He growled, giving her the opportunity to leave.

She swallowed slowly and, as he counted the seconds, her tongue swept out, wetting her bottom lip. Fletcher knew in that moment there was no going back.

For either of them.

His arms wrapped around her, his mouth slamming down on hers, and they both moaned as he took complete and absolute possession of her.

Jesus, his brain nearly exploded as he finally tasted her.

Olivia was in his arms.

Their tongues lapped and danced like their lives depended on it, taking in the taste of each other. He cupped her head as Olivia clung to his jacket and pressed her body hard against him.

Fletcher felt her hunger and was willing to feed her, but not here. He'd wanted this woman for so fucking long and this might be the only night they let down their guard and risked it.

It had to be like that.

There was no other possibility for them.

God, he wanted to lift her onto the table behind them, pull up her dress and feel just how wet she was.

And he knew by the way she felt in his arms he'd want to do it more than once.

Dammit.

Eventually, the need to breathe took dominance and their mouths parted. Panting, they stared at each other.

"Holy shit," Olivia said, touching her lips.

"You need this," Fletcher said, gruffly. "*I* need this." His fingers dusted the skin at her neck, and she shivered. "I'm done denying this, Liv."

"It's not that simple." Her nails pierced through his shirt as she clenched her fingers. "There are things you don't know."

What?

He took her chin. "Tell me."

"Sammy…"

"I've met Sammy. You know that." He frowned, confused. "We can go to my place."

She shook her head and began to pull away.

"Stop," he ordered her.

He needed more information.

"If this is about your job, I promise I will ensure we're discreet, and no one finds out." He wondered for a split second if he really could, then shook his head.

No, he would absolutely protect her.

But he had to have her. Not because he needed sex. This was more. His cock was desperate to be inside her, and he was experienced enough with women to see the painful need in Olivia's eyes.

"It's not that. Well, it is. But its… I just can't. We can't." Olivia's forehead dropped to his chest and his heart missed a beat.

"Liv." He softened his tone, his hand cupping her head. Slowly, she lifted her head, and he stared down into her blue eyes. "Please talk to me."

His phone beeped.

"Ignore it. Talk to me." He dropped his lips to hers more gently this time. She kissed him back. "I promise this will remain our secret. Nobody needs to find out. Or, if you feel like I'm pressuring you, I will stop. Immediately."

"No," she said, and her eyes turned serious. "I do want you, Fletcher. You can feel that."

He nodded.

God, could he ever.

He waited, sensing she wasn't finished talking.

She let out a sigh.

"My ex-husband. He took my daughter from me once, and could do it again."

Fletcher frowned. "I feel like I'm missing something. How is your sex life any of his business?"

Olivia sighed.

"It's a long story, but he's out there right now with his new wife, watching my every move."

Fletcher felt his body tense into a protective mode he didn't know he had. "Has he threatened you?"

She nodded, dropping her eyes.

"Tonight?" He growled.

Another nod.

Fletcher cursed. "What's he doing here?"

"He's a reporter. So's his wife."

"Name?" When she hesitated, he growled. "Olivia, his name."

She let out a long sigh and glanced toward the windows. Clearly, she was terrified of this man. Then he recalled her reaction to the photographer earlier.

"Was he the man who photographed us?" Not that he'd be able to point the guy out in a lineup, but it would explain her reaction.

He waited patiently. She would either trust him or she wouldn't.

"Yes, but there's nothing you can do, Fletcher," Olivia replied. "I just need you to understand why we can't do this. That, and it's a breach of my employment contract."

God damn policy.

He ran his thumb over her bottom lip. "I'm taking you home. We can talk there. That kiss? I'm not walking away from that, and neither should you."

"Fletcher, I've just explained. He's out there. If he sees me leave with you, he'll…"

He halted her words with a look.

"We'll leave as a group. Dakota is my date, so no one will suspect anything. I'll drop her off, and then we can talk."

This asshole wasn't dictating to him. Fletcher was taking charge, and once he understood what was going on, he would help Olivia.

She stared at him for a long moment, then nodded. "Okay."

He pulled her up against him once more. "Kiss me again."

Their lips met, and his cock jumped to attention, wanting in on the action. He slid his hand down her side, over the red fabric, feeling the arch of her breasts.

She moaned against his lips, and he smiled.

"I plan to hear you whimper my name tonight, Olivia," he declared, running his finger over her forehead to push away some red tendrils. "Are your panties wet right now?"

They'd crossed the line tonight, and he wanted her to know he had no intention of backing down.

He wanted Olivia Miller.

And he was going to have her.

She cursed, her cheeks blushing.

"Shall I take a look?" he asked, his hand snaking over her hips and tugging up her dress.

"Yes, they're wet," Olivia said quickly, and he closed his eyes, letting out a groan.

"Let's get out of here."

The sooner they did, the sooner her orgasms were his. And the sooner his cock would be deep inside her.

Whoever this man was, he wasn't going to get in the way of a Dufort getting what he wanted.

A business, a deal, or a woman.

When Olivia pulled out of his arms, he saw her desire fade and anguish return. And he wondered, for the first time in his life, if he had finally met a woman he could never have.

CHAPTER EIGHT

Olivia's lips burned from his kiss. In a delicious yet terrifying way.

She wanted to touch her fingers to them and smile, but the moment she returned to the party Simon would see right through her. After all, he had been her husband and knew what desire looked like on her.

Though she had never felt the butterflies and core-clenching need she did with Fletcher.

Ever.

With anyone.

She took one look at Fletcher and saw not just hunger, but a predator ready to pounce.

"You need to tone this down, big guy," she said, straightening his shirt and jacket.

"My hotness, you mean?" He smirked.

She slapped him playfully on the chest and he caught her hand, pulling her in for a kiss again.

"Stop. I need to gather myself, and we can't go out there looking like we've been making out," Olivia said. "I mean it. You'll understand when I explain everything."

Fletcher drew in a breath, nodded at her, then took over the job of straightening himself. He ran his hand through his hair, and her ovaries did a stupid little dance.

God, she wanted to throw herself at him.

"Stop looking at me like that or I *will* bend you over that table." He growled.

"Fletcher!" Heat flooded her core.

"Yeah, like that. But much louder." He winked. "Now, if anyone asks, I've been debriefing you. Not that it's anyone's fucking business. You *are* my PR manager."

"Okay." She nodded.

Fletcher opened the door and she stepped out, putting on her business face. The two of them walked back into the event space and, as far as she could tell, nobody paid particular attention to them.

As if it was any other day.

Not the day Fletcher Dufort had destroyed her for any other man.

"Grab Thomas and Katy," he instructed. "See if they want a ride, then meet me back over by my brothers."

Luckily, the event was already winding up. Five minutes later, she was walking across the floor with Katy, to where Fletcher stood with Dakota, Harper, and his brothers. Harper greeted her with a quick hug.

"I saw your engagement photos. You looked gorgeous," Olivia gushed.

"Thank you. It's all so overwhelming," Harper replied. "I'd love to take you up on the offer of media training, if that's still available."

"Absolutely. I'll give you a call next week to set something up. In the meantime, *no comment,* along with a pleasant smile, is your first tip."

Harper grinned.

"Looking forward to it. Maybe we can do lunch too? Oh God, sorry, I sound so desperate for friends." Harper palmed her forehead.

Olivia let out a small, friendly laugh. "I'd love to. It must be hard moving halfway across the world."

"So hard. But he's worth it." Harper gazed at Daniel with the look of a woman deeply in love.

Olivia felt a pang of envy but was happy for them both.

"Let's do the two things separately. Restaurants have ears."

"Is that tip number two?"

"Yes." Olivia laughed again and felt Fletcher step in beside her.

"Let's go." He leaned down to kiss Harper on the cheek. "Spot you later, sunshine."

Olivia smiled at the warm interaction between him and his future sister-in-law.

"Remember the new rule," Harper said to him.

"Yeah, yeah, no turning up unannounced anymore, so you can walk around naked and bang on every surface." He rolled his eyes.

"Dude," Daniel growled.

Olivia sniggered and glanced at Katy who was wide-eyed at the interaction.

"We're off. I'm dropping my team home," Fletcher said, placing his hand in the small of Dakota's back and walking off with a wave back to Daniel and Harper.

Katy and Olivia followed them. She hated watching the man who had just kissed the life out of her touching another woman so intimately.

She had no right to feel like this, but she did, and it was a worry. Fletcher was not a man she could ever be with, and she needed to get over him and prepare to see many more women on his arm.

They slipped inside the black limousine and, after dropping Katy off, they made their way back uptown toward Dakota's apartment. When it became obvious they were dropping her off next, the wealthy socialite's eyes slowly moved over to Olivia and stayed there.

Olivia held the woman's speculative stare until it was uncomfortable, then she turned to Fletcher.

Just as he started to speak, Dakota interrupted.

"I have an early start in the morning."

Fletcher nodded, looking relieved. "I understand."

Olivia sat barely breathing during the awkward ride, until they finally arrived at Dakota's building. Fletcher walked her to the door, kissed her on the cheek, then climbed back inside the limousine.

Finally, they were alone.

He stared at her across the space. His face, body and eyes were so familiar to her and yet this felt new and electric.

"That was horrible."

"It was unfair of me to do that to her," he said, his eyes dropping momentarily. "But you're important."

Olivia felt a tug in her chest. She realized, and not for the first time, that few people knew the real Fletcher Dufort. Playboy of Manhattan he might be, but he was not a shallow rich kid.

He had depth and a big heart.

He was just very selective about who he allowed to see that side of him.

When they arrived at her brownstone, Fletcher instructed Frederick to head home.

A shiver ran through her body. Did he think he was staying? Did she want him to?

Hell yes, but he couldn't.

Firstly, Sammy was inside.

Secondly, if just his kisses had her all tangled up, going further was going to complicate things even more.

He'd just have to Uber home after they talked. And had one or two more kisses.

Then it would be over.

Back to being his employee.

"Wait, I have a sitter, so just give me a minute. I'd rather she not meet you," Olivia said.

Fletcher nodded and climbed back into the limousine.

She raced inside, paid the young woman, and then stood on the doorstep watching the sitter walk back to her house, which was several doors away.

Fletcher climbed back out of the vehicle, looking every inch the powerful billionaire. He took the steps slowly, one by one, his eyes never leaving hers, then enveloped her in his arms.

Her entire body flared to life, and all sense left her.

Fletcher moved them inside, his lips slamming down on hers as the door closed behind them.

She melted into him as he pulled her flush against his body. Both of them moaned as their kiss deepened.

Holy shit, she was kissing Fletcher inside her house.

"Fuck, I've wanted to kiss you like this for months. Fucking months." He growled, walking them further into the house.

"We have to be a bit quiet," she said, kissing his lips over and over as he pushed the strap of her dress off her shoulder.

Fletcher nodded and lifted her onto the dining table, pressing his body between her legs. Her dress dipped and exposed one of her breasts.

"Jesus." His mouth surrounded her nipple and she let out a muffled moan.

Talking.

They had to talk.

"Wait, wait," she said. "I... fuck... God, Fletcher, I need to tell you everything first."

His fingers slid between her thighs and ran along the edge of her panties. "Tell me to stop."

Her body shuddered as she tried to find the will to say the words.

She didn't want him to stop.

She'd imagined this so many damn times and now finally his hands and mouth were on her.

"Fuck, you're wet." His fingers slid under the silk. "Jesus, Liv."

She gasped as he came in contact with her most sensitive part, her body blazing as he yanked her panties off, tossing them aside.

She throbbed with need as his eyes met hers, her body trembling at his predatory look.

"This. This can't happen." She spoke in one last pathetic attempt.

"It is happening, Liv, and I need you to stop resisting. You want this. Tell me you want it."

"One time. Just once."

Fletcher slowed, held her eyes for a moment, then nodded.

"Bedroom," he said, and she pointed across the room to a door.

Fletcher picked her up, nudged the door with his foot, and lay her on the bed. He tugged her dress off and then ripped his jacket off, tossing it across the room. When he removed his bow tie, she tore at the buttons of his shirt.

Then she saw what was underneath.

Holy hell.

Layers of muscle shone back at her. There was a sexy dusting of hair on his chest, but otherwise he was smooth and perfect. Those green eyes glowed as they ran over her body while he undid his black pants.

Olivia almost orgasmed on the spot when his cock sprung free. He was commando.

Good to know.

It would make every day at the office even more unbearable. God help her.

She took in his thickness, which was already dripping with pre-cum, watching as Fletcher ran his hand up and down its length.

"Let me see you." He nudged her legs apart. Trembling, she widened for him. His fingers resumed their earlier job. "So pink and wet. Beautiful."

Olivia arched into his touch, needing more.

She needed to do this.

She wanted to do this.

Just once.

Then, with their chemistry sated, she could explain why this could never happen again and they had to return to their professional relationship.

So if this was the only time she'd have with Fletcher Dufort, she was going to make the most of it.

He leaned over her, palm flat on the mattress beside her head, taking her mouth once more. "Relax, Liv. It's me."

"I know," she whispered. "God, I know."

"I'm going to make you feel amazing. Okay?"

"Yes."

Fletcher slid down her body, his soft lips sucking each nipple, as his large palm caressed her stomach and moved further to spread her legs wider. Then he was at her core and in one long slick lap he tasted her entire pussy.

She shot off the bed, but two strong hands gripped her and then his teeth nipped at her clit.

"Fuckkkingholyshit."

"You like that?"

Was he joking?

She loved every damn thing he did.

When she moaned, unable to speak, he smirked. "Good girl."

Fletcher continued nipping, sucking, and then dipping inside her like a dance until she could no longer hold back. Her fingers clutched the linen on the bed as her body convulsed.

"Come for me, Olivia. Give me all your juices," he demanded, and she cried out his name, hoping like hell she didn't wake her child.

CHAPTER NINE

Fletcher gave Olivia a moment to catch her breath as he slid the condom onto his cock. He cupped her cheek, enjoying with great pride the pleasure glowing all over her face.

She was fucking gorgeous.

He'd been with a lot of women in his life, but never had he needed to be inside one like he did right now.

As if he'd die if he couldn't.

"You still with me?" he asked with a cocky smile. His hand ran down her body, tweaking her nipple and she gasped as if in a drug-like state.

He was her drug, and he loved it.

"Yes." She arched into him.

Thank fuck.

Fletcher lowered his lips to hers and pulled her legs around him. Then, as he pressed to her entrance, their eyes connected. Like a sonic boom, as he inched inside her, he felt their souls connect.

He wanted to howl out his animalistic appreciation as he sunk deep into the heart of her tight, hot femininity.

"Jesus." He growled.

He felt a frenzy come over him, driving him to pound her, while wanting to nurture her, please her. Yet he found the strength to pull out and slide back in, learning her body.

"You feel incredible," he ground out, consumed by the feel of her wrapped around his cock.

"I'm going to come again." She panted. "How is that possible?"

He smiled, brushing hair from her forehead in a haphazard way as he thrust faster, not taking his eyes from hers.

His cock swelled.

The fierce, blazing fire their bodies were creating was more intense than anything he'd ever felt.

"Don't hold back, gorgeous. I want to feel your pleasure while you clench around my cock. Take all you need."

She threw back her head and her nails dug into his wide shoulders, crying out his name. He drove deeper and sped up as she tightened and slid over his thick, hard member.

"Oh, fuck, Liv." He cried out his own orgasm as their bodies spasmed and shook as one.

Never had he come so hard and fast in his life.

Fletcher gazed down at Olivia with absolute awe as his body throbbed in the aftermath of such bliss.

She was glowing like a goddess. A completely wiped-out goddess. He gently pulled out and collapsed beside her.

"Come here." Fletcher pulled her into his arms for a few minutes before heading to the bathroom to deposit the condom and returning with a cloth for her.

She blushed and he let out a small laugh.

"I've had my mouth on you and this embarrasses you?"

"It's different." She batted his hand away, taking over the job.

"How?"

"I don't know." She laughed. "Just more… intimate."

"More so than sex?"

"Intimacy isn't just sex, Fletch. When you get married, you'll understand." For some reason, her comment irritated him.

"Ouch."

"Sorry. That sounded a bit superior, didn't it? Trust me, being married is not all it's made out to be."

On that, they agreed totally.

He flopped back on the bed and pulled her into his arms again.

When?

She'd said *when* he married.

Fletcher was surprised by that. Most women were angling for a relationship with him by this point, not directing the conversation away from them toward him marrying someone else.

"I want intimacy with you," Fletcher suddenly said, the words falling out before he could stop them.

But he realized he meant them.

He cupped her chin and pressed his lips on hers with more pressure than was necessary. As if his mouth was an exclamation point or something.

"And I want to do that again. Like fifty more times."

Olivia smiled sadly.

What the hell?

Did she not feel their connection?

How was she not blown away by what they had just shared? He'd felt it to his very core.

"We should talk." She pulled the sheets over them as if they were some kind of shield.

He frowned while she let out a sigh.

"I know. I just wanted to enjoy this a little longer."

She gave him another of those damn sad smiles.

Fletcher shifted to face her, so she knew she had his attention.

"Three years ago, I left my then husband, Simon. He was abusive. Subtly at first, and then one day I watched a movie where the main character was being gaslit by her fiancé." She glanced at him. "It's embarrassing to admit, because I consider myself an intelligent woman, but that's the thing about gaslighting; it's slow and harmful. It makes you question yourself and your sanity."

Fletcher had heard a bit about gaslighting, but he wasn't an expert.

"Is it the same as narcissism?"

"They tend to go hand in hand. He is also a narcissist. They're incapable of seeing their behavior in a negative way, so they'll never change. When I learned more about it, I realized the only choice I had was to leave. While it's a result of pain from a person's childhood, it doesn't mean you should stay and put up with the abuse. Nor subject Sammy to it."

"Hell no," he said firmly.

"I knew it would be a rough few months, but I thought if I could create at least one safe home for Sammy, then it would be better than if she lived with him full time. I could lessen the damage, you know."

God, she was amazing.

He had known Olivia for two years. He already knew she was strong, but listening to her story he realized she was very different to his mother.

Marie Dufort had stayed with their father even when she knew he was sleeping with other women. Even when she knew others were aware of it.

When their father had relocated her to another house and divorced her, she remained bitter.

Fletcher strongly believed that you taught people how you wanted to be treated. Every time their father had stayed out with another woman, and she'd said nothing, it was telling his dad that the behavior was okay.

He knew she knew. And she knew he knew, she knew.

So fucked up.

Every time his mother looked in the mirror knowing her husband was being disloyal, and did nothing, she was telling the world—and more importantly, herself—that she didn't deserve to be loved, honored, and respected.

And that was never true.

Not for anyone.

Fletcher believed it was every single person's job to demand love and respect by setting boundaries and protecting those boundaries every single day.

Olivia had done that by leaving her abusive husband. Damn, he respected her for that. Plus, it told him she wasn't a woman he could play with.

"You should be proud of yourself for having so much courage." He brushed a lock of red hair off her face.

The corner of her lip lifted, cynically.

"Well, unfortunately, things didn't go quite to plan."

Oh?

Fletcher felt a chill run through him.

Olivia chewed her bottom lip as her eyes darted around the room. It was a risk telling Fletcher her full story.

He may be her lover right now, but he was first and foremost her employer. If he didn't believe her, and learned she'd been accused of having drugs in her possession and of being a drug user, she could lose her job.

It was a real possibility.

Her career was hanging by a thread right now so, regardless of the mind blowing, delicious and incredible sex they'd just had, she had to carefully consider her next move.

She fiddled with the sheet.

"Hey," Fletch said, taking her hand. "Tell me."

"He took Sammy from me," she replied.

Just saying those words out loud brought up all the emotions from the past.

Tears of fury and sadness filled her eyes.

Dammit.

She didn't want to be so emotional in front of him, but he needed to know why she couldn't be in an open relationship with him. Not because of the anti-fraternization policy at Dufort Hotels, but because of the very real risk in her life.

While they had agreed to one time earlier, Olivia had a feeling Fletcher wanted more.

It couldn't happen.

Despite lying beside him right now and wishing she could have more of the handsome, sexy, and incredible man, this one moment was all she could allow.

Even this was a hell of a risk.

And yet she couldn't regret it after the heavenly orgasms he'd given her.

"What the hell? How?" Fletcher asked, his voice rising.

She shushed him, pointing to the wall, toward Sammy's room.

"She's just in there. Quiet," she said.

"Sorry, but what the fuck?" He spoke more quietly.

She nodded knowingly at him.

What the fuck, all right.

"He was sleeping with my friend Emma, and the two of them set me up. She brought Molly into my house and drugged my coffee," Olivia explained. "They fell out of her handbag and she said they belonged to a friend. When she was called away on an urgent story—she's a reporter—I stupidly put them in a cupboard so Sammy couldn't get into them."

Fletcher shook his head.

"Simon turned up just as the drugs kicked in and called CPC. An hour later, they took my daughter," she added, emotion rich in her voice.

"Fuck, Liv." A cry escaped her throat. He pulled her into his arms and, for the first time since it had all happened, she felt supported in a way she didn't know had been missing.

Like she could let go and truly cry.

And she did.

His strong arms around her felt protective and safe from the harsh untrustworthy world she'd been living in.

She knew it was temporary but let herself go, knowing Fletcher was a good man.

She sniffed and sat up. "Thank you."

"For what?"

"Just," she laughed snottily, "for the hug."

Fletcher shook his head. "Liv, this is bad. Who is this guy?"

"He's a reporter," she replied. "He's not out of my life and won't be for another twelve years. My lawyer got me shared custody of Sammy, but it took six long agonizing months, Fletch. Every day he torments me with threats to take her away again."

Fletcher cursed.

She needed him to understand the seriousness of her situation. Truly understand.

"He saw us together tonight and asked if we were sleeping together. No, that's incorrect. He accused me of fucking you. I have to be careful. He'll use anything to discredit and hurt me."

"No, we have to deal with him. This is no way for you to live, Olivia. Fuck that. I won't have him doing this to you." He growled.

We?

She shook her head and closed her eyes.

"You don't understand. He's Sammy's father. He'll never be gone from my life *and* anything I do could backfire on me... and more importantly, her. I don't know if he'd hurt her, but I just can't take the risk."

Fletcher leaped out of bed and began cursing and pacing the floor. She tucked her knees up and wrapped her arms around them.

"No," he said. "There has to be..."

She waited for him to connect the dots and realize, as she had, that it was hopeless.

"He's not above the law. He's a damn reporter. We'll…"

It always came back around to Sammy. Whatever they did to Simon, she would be the one to suffer the consequences.

"Jesus," he groaned.

She didn't bother lifting her head. She just nodded, staring at the mattress. He climbed back on the bed and pulled her into his arms.

"I don't have the answers right now, but I am going to do everything in my power to help you. I… I'm not letting him destroy your life any more than he has. I know people. Powerful people."

She lifted her hand to cup his cheek and smiled sadly.

"There's nothing you can do, but I appreciate you caring."

He tugged her harder against him.

"Liv, I'm not going to sit back and do nothing. Don't even ask that of me. You should know that's not who I am. That's not what the Dufort family does."

Oh, shit.

Her eyes widened. She'd totally overlooked Fletcher's nature. His lifestyle.

Of course, he wasn't going to let this go. He was a powerful man who didn't have a clue how powerless some people were.

This wasn't something he could fix, but as he'd said, he wasn't going to let it go.

He had to.

Fletcher and all the Dufort men were powerful, but they didn't have children. They didn't understand the consequences of losing a child.

Her heart began to pound.

The last thing she wanted was for the two of them to get so entangled in this desire they had for each other that it destroyed their lives.

She had to draw a strong line in the sand, so he knew where the boundaries were.

"Fletch, stop. The reason I told you about this was so you would understand why we can't be involved. Even if Daniel changed the company policy, I still can't be with you.

"You're too well known, and the media follow your love life like a pack of hyenas. Simon would find out and then… well, I could lose Sammy."

His jaw stiffened.

She ran her hand down his arm and let her eyes soften as they drifted back to his. "You said you wanted to do that fifty more times. I don't know if I can do that many, but I have a few more rounds in me until morning."

Fletcher groaned. "I'm not letting this—"

"Yes, you are. But you don't need to let me go just yet," she said, as his body shifted and he tugged her underneath him.

Olivia gave him a sexy smile.

Tomorrow she'd be grieving the loss of what could never be between them.

Fletcher was everything she wanted in a man. He was smart, funny, successful, protective, and caring.

She just hoped he wouldn't poke the bear that was her ex-husband. She didn't want to regret this night with Fletcher.

CHAPTER TEN

Fletcher had slipped out just as the sun rose, before plastering Olivia with kisses, and promising to call her over the weekend.

She'd told him not to.

He had given her a frown, and it concerned her that he hadn't fully understood the risks.

What was clear, though, even if she didn't want to face it, was their chemistry was off the charts.

But if he called, she couldn't ignore him. He was her boss and her job meant being available twenty-four-seven in the situation of a media crisis.

She had jumped in the shower and changed into PJs, then climbed back into bed moments before Sammy zombie-walked into her bedroom.

"Mom," her sweet little voice croaked, sliding in next to her and curling into her chest.

"Morning, darling." She kissed Sammy's forehead. "Did you have fun with Lizzy last night?"

Sammy nodded sleepily, not ready to share details of her evening with the babysitter.

Any moment now Sammy would transform into a little firecracker, bouncing around the room at a million miles an hour, so Olivia just lay there, closing her eyes, taking in the last moments of peace and quiet until bedtime.

She never wished her daughter away, like she saw other parents on social media joking about. She *totally* got it, but after experiencing six months without her, Olivia spent every single day with Sammy counting her blessings. If it meant she had to drag herself through the day on little sleep, she was happy to do that.

Plus, the reason she'd missed out on sleep was not something she was complaining about at all. Her body was aching in places it hadn't for a long time. And never like this.

Fletcher had been more than she had ever imagined. And she'd done a lot of imagining over the past year. The way he'd focused on her body and pleasure, the way his familiar green eyes had searched deep within her as he joined their bodies, had been overwhelming and yet perfect.

So damn perfect.

But that was it.

They had had their delicious sexy moments together and now they had to move on.

Sadness floated through her.

At least she would see him at work, but there would be pros and cons to that. Still, not having Fletcher in her life, ever, was not something she was ready for.

She'd need to get over him fast. It wouldn't take long before he was in the media with another woman, whether it was real or not, and Olivia didn't have the luxury of being able to turn off the news.

It was her job to be on top of it.

Damn it.

"Mom, can we go to the park?" Sammy's head suddenly popped up, and then she was off.

She scrambled out of the sheets, her little legs kicking, and began jumping up and down, giggling and telling stories about her evening with Lizzy.

Olivia climbed out of bed, threw on a robe, and walked into the kitchen, turning on the coffee maker while nodding and making all the right noise responses, so Sammy thought she was listening.

She was.

Mostly.

"Cereal or pancakes?"

"Pancakes!" Sammy answered, clapping. "Chocolate." When Olivia frowned, Sammy sighed. "Okay, fine, blueberry."

"Go make your bed and they'll be ready when you're finished," she called as her daughter raced off.

She'd have to remake the bed, but Olivia was trying to teach her good habits. It felt like every week she was making leeway by Sunday when Sammy went to her father's place, only to have her return with bad habits the following weekend.

At least she returned.

Olivia figured it was about being consistent with her and at the end of the day, Sammy would decide who she wanted to be. There was a lot of loving and letting go in parenting that she had never imagined before becoming one.

Unfortunately, she'd chosen a horrible man to procreate with, but she couldn't regret it when she looked at her daughter. She loved Sammy more than her own breath.

Which is why, she reminded herself, she had to be smart about Fletcher.

The itch was scratched, and now it was time to move on.

She would talk to Fletcher on Monday to be sure he wasn't going to do anything to jeopardize her shared custody arrangement or trigger Simon.

Olivia knew she was likely being a little paranoid, and that Simon had few legs to stand on when it came to many of his threats, but he'd lied under oath, planted drugs *and* drugged her to get Sammy once.

She wasn't going to let her barriers down for a second.

Did she dream of going into protective custody and never having him in her life again?

You bet!

Was it possible? No.

Because her life wasn't a Hollywood fiction movie.

Dammit.

If that was the case, she'd get the guy and a life without Simon.

Narcissists were dangerous. They had no conscience paired with a willingness to lie and do whatever it took to win.

So she had to be one step ahead.

Sammy needed her. Every day they'd been apart over those horrific six months had been a nightmare. Olivia had imagined the most terrible things which may or may not be true. She'd tried to ask Sammy about what life was like with her father, but carefully. The last thing she wanted was her daughter repeating the questions, innocently, and having that backfiring on her.

But the thing was, narcissistic behaviors were often invisible to the outside world; the scars unseen, the damage impossible to prove in a courtroom.

He could be doing so much damage to Sammy emotionally and mentally, and there was nothing she could do.

Her fists clenched against the kitchen bench.

Now she had fifty percent custody, Olivia was able to reduce the exposure Sammy had with her father and try to counter it with her love. She constantly told her daughter how amazing and beautiful she was, and how she could be anything she wanted.

It wasn't perfect, but it was better than nothing.

After breakfast, she dragged Sammy to the shops for a new pair of school shoes, and then they went to the park and met Addison and Sienna.

Addison was the only friend who'd genuinely believed she wasn't guilty when Sammy had been taken from her.

"You, take drugs? No offense, but you're too straight-laced for that," Addison had joked.

"Hey, I'm not... okay, maybe I am." Olivia had shrugged, then burst into tears at the relief of someone believing her.

She'd also introduced her to Belinda Pendleton—the lawyer who had helped her get Sammy back.

It had deepened their friendship and if Addison ever needed anything, Olivia was the first person to put up her hand to help. Not because she felt indebted, but because true friends were a rare and valuable commodity.

Liv had moved around a lot when she was younger due to being an army brat. When her father died, her mother had moved them to New York, and she'd met Addison at high school.

They both worked in the marketing field and had seen each other marry, have children, and divorce.

Though Addison's ex-husband wasn't a psycho, so there was that.

"What's up today? You look tired," Addison said.

"We had the opening of the SoHo Dufort last night."

"Oh, that's right. How did it go?"

Olivia was tempted to tell her what had happened between her and Fletcher, but the fear ran deep when it came to Simon. She didn't think Addison would ever tell anyone, but all it would take was one little slip, and she could lose Sammy.

"Really good, but these things go late, so I'm running on empty today." She tucked her legs under her as they sat on the grass watching the girls try to throw a frisbee.

Olivia had found it in the toy shop earlier in the day, and it had made her smile, reminding her of her childhood. Sammy thought it was a plastic plate, so they'd had to show the girls how it worked.

Watching them toss it and then see it fall flat in front of them was just another funny flashback.

"Throw it up in the air diagonally, like we showed you," Addison called out. "Not straight up into the sky."

"This is dumb," Sammy said, picking it up grumpily and trying again.

"So dumb," Sienna, who was a year older, mumbled.

Olivia cast Addison a glance, and they tried to hide their sniggers. She'd been expecting the girls to lose interest pretty quickly. They'd be asking for their iPads soon enough.

Her phone beeped. It was Fletcher.

Shit.

She grappled to get her phone from the grass in front of her.

"He messages you a lot on the weekends," Addison observed.

Olivia blushed and tried to brush away her reaction.

"Weekends?" she repeated. "Yes. No. Oh, it's probably because of last night," she stumbled out, and Addison frowned at her.

She swiped and read the text, staring at it.

I can't stop thinking of you, dammit. Fletch x

Her entire body buzzed with excitement. She couldn't meet Addison's eyes—her friend would see right through her. She cleared her throat and nodded, hoping it would appear like she was thinking about business stuff.

She locked the phone, put it in her handbag and took a swig of water from her bottle.

Addison stared at her. "Bad?"

Yes, it was bad.

Very bad.

Both of them were supposed to have shagged and not looked back.

Instead, she'd spent the day thinking about the way he'd touched her and run his tongue through her swollen needy flesh. She wanted to feel his delicious touch again, but it wasn't possible.

Sleeping with Fletcher had only made both of them want more.

He wants me.

Part of her soared with joy knowing that.

Who could blame her? Fletcher Dufort was absolutely gorgeous, rich, and adorable.

And he wanted her!

She thought herself lucky to get the job working with him at Dufort Hotels two years ago. Now he wanted her sexually.

Olivia let herself take a little moment to revel in the fact.

Then she shook it off.

Neither of them had a chance at being together, whether it was casual or otherwise. Dufort didn't allow relationships, and Fletcher couldn't exactly leave his own family's company. And she couldn't afford to lose her job.

If she did, Simon would use that as fodder to get full custody of Sammy. He wouldn't have to pull another illegal stunt. She would all but hand her daughter over to him.

"He's just worried about some of the press. I can deal on Monday," she said.

It would be better if she didn't respond.

Olivia decided to ignore his message and let him know she was serious about last night being a one-time deal.

CHAPTER ELEVEN

Fletcher slammed his hand down on the stop button of his treadmill and cursed. He jumped off and grabbed the towel, wiping his forehead, and stared out at the Manhattan skyline.

The clear blue sky did nothing to improve his mood. After sleeping with Olivia last night he thought he'd be flying high.

No.

All he wanted was more of her.

He'd tried to do a few hours of work earlier and ended up gazing out the window, trying to come up with a solution to the asshole ex-husband problem.

He'd come up dry.

Who took a child away from an incredible woman like Olivia? What a sick fucker.

Fletcher had met enough narcissists in business over the years to know the kind of man this Simon was. They were hard to spot initially, but when you started negotiations with them, they soon showed their true colors.

Daniel was a master at messing with them.

He'd love to speak to his older brother and get advice, but Dan would see right through his questioning. Even his brother's new fiancée wasn't enough to distract him from what he *thought* was going on between him and Olivia.

Okay, fine—what *was* going on between them.

Fletcher understood the risks for Olivia and was taking it seriously. He'd met Sammy, and she was a gorgeous little girl. No child should be without its mother.

But could he stand back and let some asshole manipulate an innocent woman?

Unlikely.

He knew he should step away and focus on getting their relationship back to a professional one. He should find someone to distract him. Someone sexy and... someone who wasn't the forbidden fruit in every way.

Fletcher thought, by tasting Olivia, he would quench his hunger.

The opposite had happened.

Now he just wanted more of her, as if she was his very own drug of choice.

Those dark pink nipples, her moist pussy, her swollen ready lips—they kept flashing through his mind and tempting him like the devil. Closing his eyes, he could nearly feel the moment his fingers slid inside her as she arched, needing and wanting more.

Christ, she was a sensual, sexy goddess, with her flaming red hair spread around her as her mouth parted. It was the perfect invite for his cock.

How could he not want more?

Was he going to let some fucktard reporter stop him from having Olivia again?

No fucking way.

The company policy? Well, that was a little trickier.

He grabbed his phone from the top of the cabinet in his gymnasium and checked his texts.

No answer.

Damn her.

Fletcher knew what she was doing.

Olivia was sending him a clear message.

She'd been very clear she was scared to lose Sammy, and he respected that. The difference between someone powerful, wealthy, and successful like him and average folk was that he didn't let fear rule his life.

Fear blocked you from being able to see the possibilities available to you. And usually there were many options if you just looked.

Olivia could only see the trap Simon had stuck her in.

Fletcher was going to start looking for other options. He would find a way to protect both Liv and Sammy, and deal with this Simon dick.

The answer would come.

It had to. It appeared that he wanted more of her, so he wasn't going to let Simon stop him. He'd go out of his mind if he couldn't taste her again.

But it was more than that. This was Olivia. He wanted to talk to her, hold her in his arms again and listen to her laugh and tell him stories.

Knowing she was trapped by this fucker was making him furious.

He'd meant it when he told her the Dufort family didn't sit by idly and let people push them around. The US senator who'd tried to blackmail Daniel not long ago had found that out the hard way.

He'd failed.

Daniel had used a private security company who may be able to help Olivia. She'd made it clear she didn't want his help, but Fletcher knew that was her fear talking.

He just had to be careful.

Fletcher quickly showered, turned off the jets, and then stepped out, staring at his reflection in the mirror. He ran a hand over his pec, down his abdomen, and gripped his cock.

One phone call and he could have any number of New York women on their knees and sucking him off this evening.

Instead, he had other plans.

CHAPTER TWELVE

Olivia put down the book and kissed Sammy gently on the forehead.

Finally.

She was dead on her feet and ready to go to bed herself, even though it was only seven thirty.

She switched off the light and made sure Sammy's little unicorn night light was glowing, then pulled the door closed.

Olivia eyed the sofa for a long moment, and her half-drunk glass of wine and contemplated whether she'd be able to stay awake long enough to finish it. Or if she'd wake up with a crook neck at three in the morning, cold on the sofa.

It wouldn't be the first time.

Only this time it wasn't from working late or doing a last-minute school costume, it was from a sleepless sexy night with a rich, handsome bachelor.

A once-in-a-lifetime moment.

Olivia had begun thinking she'd have to leave Dufort Hotels eventually after what they'd done. Perhaps not straight away, but sooner rather than later. She trusted, in the meantime, she and Fletcher could find a comfortable place to work together for a little while longer.

Despite his text.

Now her mind was reeling. She decided to sit down and finish her wine.

God, how she wanted to reply and tell him she was feeling the same way. Half of her was focused on doing the right thing while the other half wanted to feel his lips on hers, his strong warm arms around her. It felt so nice to be touched again.

Touched by Fletcher.

It had been twelve long months of sexual tension building between them, so it was no wonder they both wanted more. That, and it had been absolutely incredible.

Perhaps it would just take time for them to put it behind them.

Her phone, which was on silent, lit up with a message. She frowned, knowing who it was before she even looked.

Open the door.

What?

Knock, knock.

The hell?

He was not outside her door, was he?

Olivia jumped off the sofa and ran over, peering through her peephole.

"Open the door, Liv," Fletcher commanded.

No, no, no.

She glanced down at her black sweatpants and old Led Zeppelin t-shirt and tugged on her hair which was in a half pony-half messy bun.

AKA: a damn mess.

She had zero makeup on and smelled like chocolate cookies, which she'd baked earlier for Sammy's playdate tomorrow afternoon.

"Fletch, what are you doing here?" she asked in a low voice.

"Are you going to let me in?"

"No."

She heard him curse and bit back a laugh, nibbling her bottom lip. A part of her was thrilled he was here, even though she knew he shouldn't be.

"Liv, open the damn door," Fletcher said, and when she looked again, she saw his arm leaning on the doorframe, and holy hell, his biceps were so damn sexy even warped through the peephole.

She let out a sigh and slid the lock open.

As soon as the door moved an inch, Fletcher pushed it open, closed it behind him, then glanced around. She knew who he was looking for.

"She's in bed," Olivia said, then a second later, his body enveloped hers, and his mouth smashed down on hers.

When they parted, they were both panting and smiling at each other like idiots.

"Hi," he smirked.

"What are you doing here?" she laughed.

"That," Fletcher replied. "And this." He kissed her again, sliding his fingers into her bird's nest of hair.

She moaned.

God damn, the man was sex on two legs and knew it. But he couldn't be here. What if Simon had seen him?

Not that she thought even *he* was evil enough to sit staking out her house, watching her every move.

Probably.

"I needed to see you," Fletcher said, staring down at her with glossy eyes. "Before we go back to the office on Monday, I wanted to see you again. Plus, you never replied to my text."

"I didn't know what to say."

"Were you thinking about me?" He ran his thumb along her lip.

"Of course I was." She nodded, shivering under his touch. "But we agreed, just one night."

"I'm not sure that was a solid agreement. I never signed anything." He shrugged and smirked at her.

"Fletcher Dufort. This isn't one of your business deals." She shook her head, grinning at him even though she was well aware of the position he was putting her in.

It was hard to be mad when she was wrapped up in six foot two inches of solid, sexy muscle.

"No, but nevertheless I'm pretty sure I was distracted and not in a position to be making a sound decision."

"So, the court of Fletcher throws it out?"

"Exactly."

She laughed.

It was the type of banter they usually had sitting around a desk, not standing in his arms while he looked ready to ravish her again.

God help her, she could fall for this man if she wasn't careful. She slipped out of his arms and glanced around, then down at herself, wishing she'd worn something a little less sloppy.

"I wasn't expecting company. Do you want a glass of wine?"

"Sure," he replied.

She poured him a glass, looking up briefly as Fletcher stood in the middle of her home.

He looked as confident as ever, but completely out of place. She didn't know what it was, but it probably had something to do with the fact his jeans cost more than her sofa, and his huge watch more than her entire apartment.

Fletcher was a billionaire.

She may work with him every day, but seeing him inside her home, outside the lust-filled haze they'd shared last night, she was reminded how very different they were.

"It's just from Wholefoods. Nothing fancy." She handed him the glass.

"It's fine, it's…" He winced as he took a sip, smiled, and put it down on the coffee table as they both sat on the sofa. "Okay, it's pretty bad."

His expensive tastes wouldn't be satisfied here. Except, apparently, what they did in the bedroom. She shook her head, but was soon distracted as he reached out and tugged her against him.

"Fletch," she warned softly.

His free hand landed on her thigh, and she realized hers had done the same. Like two pieces of a puzzle slipping into place.

She gazed into his gorgeous green eyes in an attempt to look growly.

"Olivia," he smirked.

"It was just one night," she repeated.

Forget the other barriers to their forbidden relationship, Olivia was worried her heart was going to get broken by this heart throb of a man.

"Let's make it two."

God damn him.

He reached to brush her hair away and like a magnet she leaned into him, their lips meeting for a lazy long core-melting kiss.

"You taste like raspberries," he moaned.

"It's my lip gloss." She pointed to one of the three raspberry lip balms she owned. One lived on her desk, which she took into meetings with her, one in her handbag and one at home.

He groaned. "I know. I've been fantasizing about that damn stuff for months."

"Really?" she asked, smiling. He nodded slowly about ten times, and her smile stretched into a grin. "Like, when we've been at work in meetings?"

Suddenly, the idea of him imagining her mouth set her body alight. It was both an incredibly naughty and delicious thought she knew was going to haunt her.

How was she going to work with him every day wondering if he was thinking these thoughts?

Her body shivered.

Fletcher tugged her under him playfully, but those green eyes of his burned intensely as he lay over her.

"Don't ask questions you don't want the answer to," he growled. "But yes, every time you ran that red stuff over your lips, my cock would…"

"Would?" she prodded, knowing she shouldn't.

"Harden at the thought of your lips wrapped around them."

Fletcher slipped his hand under her top, working his way to her cotton bra. Her nipples hardened.

They stared at each other, both lost in their flashbacks of meetings together and how that could have easily happened. They were alone often in his large private office.

"So many times I wanted to ask you to get on your knees."

Olivia swallowed.

Would she have done it?

"I imagined sliding my zipper down, pulling out my hard cock and watching your gloss-covered mouth open, eager for it."

She smirked.

"What?" he asked, surprised.

"Such a boy fantasy." She laughed.

He glowered at her in such a masculine and primal way it nearly took her breath away.

"First, I'm a man, Olivia Miller. Secondly, do I need to prove it to you again?"

She swallowed.

He had nothing to prove. Absolutely nothing, but that wasn't the question.

Did she want him again? Hell yes.

Should she?

Her panties were completely soaked, and it wouldn't take much for him to slip his hand inside her sweatpants and discover it. He knew she wanted him.

She shook her head.

"My bad. You are all man, Fletcher Dufort."

"Are you telling me you never imagined anything like that? Ever?"

She blushed.

Fletcher grinned and pinched her nipple. "Confess. Come on, tell me what girls fantasize about."

She swatted his hand away. "Woman, I'm a woman, seeing as we're getting technical here."

Fletcher returned to her nipple, and she let out a little moan.

"Continue." He grinned.

"Well… it's pretty hard to ignore how hot you are." She shook her head at his smirk. "So, it was the little things you did."

"Such as?"

God, he was the last man on earth who needed an ego boost.

"When you'd take off, or put on, your jacket. Or—"

"My jacket?" he asked, his eyes narrowing even as he grinned.

"Yes, your arms." She ran her hands over his thick biceps. "Your muscles, they stretch the fabric of your shirts and it's, well, it creates a reaction in my body."

"How? Tell me." His voice thickened.

"Heat. A hot need between my thighs," she said, as he ran his hand between them, touching her right where she had described.

He began circling her core.

"And is this what you wanted when you felt like that?"

"Yes."

"Were you in my office?"

She nodded.

"Alone with me?"

She nodded again.

"You could have sat and removed your panties. Asking me to relieve your need." He pressed harder through her sweatpants.

Shamelessly, she arched her pelvis into his hands.

"You could have leaned back on my sofa, widened your legs and let me see the glistening wetness of your pussy."

Olivia was unable to find words. God, that had been exactly what she wanted. The aching and clenching of her thighs for over twelve months during meetings had been agonizing.

Fletcher stood, and her eyes flew open.

He scooped her up and carried her into the bedroom.

"Flet—"

His finger pressed to her lips, then he quickly pulled her sweatpants and panties off, and nudged her onto the bed.

Oh, shit.

She stared up at the ceiling as his hands spread her thighs and he kneeled down between them. His mouth surrounded her pussy, and she had to shove her fist into her mouth to stay silent.

Silent-ish.

Jesus, she was in trouble.

How could she work every day with this man she desired and adored, and never want this again?

When his fingers entered her and his thumb rubbed against her clit, she grabbed a pillow and pressed it to her face.

"We're in my office, Liv," he said. "I have you spread out on my desk. I'm tasting your pussy, and someone is going to walk in."

Oh, God.

Fletcher's tongue flicked and his mouth sucked as he fucked her with his fingers. "Someone is knocking at the door, and you are spread wide."

She reached with her other hand and threaded her fingers through his hair. She was close. So close.

He stopped.

Her eyes flew open, and she pushed the pillow away. Fletcher stood and ripped open his jeans, kicking them off after tearing open a condom.

"Don't you come without me. I want to feel you around my cock," he demanded, his eyes not leaving hers. Then he pushed her up the bed a little, kneeled and gripped his cock in one hand, spreading her wetness around it.

"If this is our last time, Liv, then I want you to know how damn much I love fucking you." Fletcher pressed into her as he leaned over and took her mouth with his.

They both moaned as he filled her, inch by inch.

"Me too," she cried softly. "God, me too."

CHAPTER THIRTEEN

Fletcher closed his laptop and stood to go to his full team meeting. The full team met once a month but, Murphy's damn law, today was the day.

It was Monday morning and the first time he would see Olivia professionally since sleeping with her.

He could have moved the meeting. He was the director of marketing and PR after all.

The last thing he felt like doing was sitting in a room full of employees pretending he hadn't spent Saturday evening lapping away at Olivia's pussy. Or sunk deep inside her, wishing he could do it every night for as long as she'd let him.

Which was unusual.

He rarely spent more than one or two nights with a woman, and never consecutively. Fletcher was pretty sure the forbidden nature of being with Olivia was creating a heightened arousal that would soon fade away.

He shook his head.

That was bullshit. Just thinking about it in that way felt disloyal. He liked Olivia. As a person. Hell, he more than liked her—he cared about her. It wasn't like they'd just met. Together they had overcome challenges, created some great wins for the Dufort Hotel group, and shared failures.

Plus, yes, he fucking desired her.

Fletcher dug through his drawer for a pen, idly thinking. Procrastinating.

Delaying.

He did want her.

He wanted, if he had to, to drink cheap wine with her and feel her body under him again this weekend. And probably the next. Then he wanted to take her to his favorite restaurant and introduce her to *his* wines.

Because he wasn't a masochist and there was only so much punishment he could take.

He wanted her in his bed, on his sofa. He wanted her up against his shower wall and to hear her scream. Then wake with her in his arms.

He had to find a way to convince her it was safe to spend more time with him so they could enjoy what they had until it naturally fizzled out.

Because it would.

He didn't do serious long-term relationships. Marriage wasn't for him. Just because Daniel had fallen, it didn't mean he and Hunter would do the same.

Olivia was an incredibly beautiful and sexy woman. She was oblivious to her sexuality, and it was that quality, plus her bright, quick mind, that had his cock hardening when she'd slip on that damn raspberry lip-gloss.

Fletcher loved talking to her and watching her break into a laugh when he teased her.

Shit.

These were the thoughts that had kept him awake all last night.

She was beginning to feel important.

This was supposed to be purely sexual. An office romance of forbidden lust. Fun, sexy, naughty.

"Hey."

His head shot up and, in his doorway, stood the woman to whom he appeared to be losing his mind. Even while he was playing tennis with Hunter on Sunday, visions of her body arching under him, her mouth crying out as quietly as she'd been able, until he'd slammed his lips over hers, had distracted him.

He'd lost the tennis match.

Hunter had smirked and shaken his head, as if he knew what had thrown him off. Fortunately, he hadn't said anything.

Watching Olivia now as she stood in his doorway, recalling the way they'd said goodbye early Sunday morning before her daughter woke, triggered something within him.

Something primal and raw.

He'd asked her to spend the following weekend with him. Sammy would be at her fathers and there was no reason they couldn't enjoy a couple more days together.

She had said no.

Firmly.

He didn't know why it had bothered him so much. Yes, he wanted more of her body, but her rejection hurt.

Which was ridiculous.

He was Fletcher Dufort, Playboy of Manhattan.

So, he was torn.

Part of him wanted to break down her defenses and destroy Simon the fucker. The other part of him knew he should let it go—let her go—and go find someone else to play with.

He had to try.

"Good morning, Olivia," he said, cool and professional.

God, she looked incredible in her black skirt and green blouse. Those buttons didn't look all that secure, and the long chain that hung down between her breasts should be illegal.

He'd have to tell her it was inappropriate. It was like she had one of those giant baseball fingers pointing at her chest saying *stare at my breasts.*

His eyes ran down her tanned long legs to her black heels, which strapped around her ankles.

Fucking hell.

He coughed.

"You okay?" Olivia asked.

"Yes, why? Am I late?" he asked.

"No." She frowned, stepping further into the room.

God, no, don't do that.

"Okay, see you in there," he replied, not looking at her.

"Fletcher, I—"

"I'll see you in there, Olivia." He spoke more sternly, looking up at her.

She stared for a moment, looking disappointed in him, nodded, turned, and left.

Fuck.

Shit, fuck, shit, fuck.

Why had he done that? Did he need to be such an asshole?

Daniel stepped into the office a second later, his head swiveling to take in Olivia's back before staring at him.

"What's up?" Daniel asked.

"Nothing is fucking up. Why is everyone asking what is up? Nothing. That's what's up," he snapped.

Good one, idiot.

"Fine, you have your period. I pity your team today." Daniel ignored any social signals he should leave and propped himself on the edge of the sofa.

"And yet here you are, still standing in my office while I need to change my tampon." He walked around his desk.

Daniel let out a snort.

"I have a team meeting," he said in the hope his brother would leave.

"What timing." Daniel laughed.

"Get out," Fletcher said, standing at the door.

"Come and see me when you're finished."

"About?"

"About me being the Chief Executive Officer of Dufort Hotels, and I've asked you to meet with me," Daniel said. "Now go change your tampon and I'll see you after."

Asshole.

Working with family was a pain in the damn ass some days. On principle, he was going to be busy all morning now.

Fletcher stepped into the large meeting room, where the wider marketing team sat around the board table. It was covered with notepads and pens, phones, coffees, water bottles, and laptops.

There were around twenty-five people in the room with a dozen more dialed in via video from around the world.

Olivia was seated next to the empty chair, which was his usual spot, and staring at her tablet.

He should never have snapped at her.

Fletcher took a moment to acknowledge *this* was why the anti-fraternization policy was in place. The power imbalance was completely in his favor, and Olivia was probably, right now, concerned about her job.

She had nothing to worry about. He had been an asshole.

Damn it.

The thing was, he didn't know how to *not* want her. How could he go back to their jovial, fun working relationship when all he wanted to do was tug open her shirt and run his thumb over her nipples? How could he greet her every morning when his body wanted to tug her against him and feel her lips on his?

Everyone looked up as he closed the door.

"Good morning."

A bunch of *mornings* sounded throughout the room. Some chirpy, some mumbled.

He sat.

"Before we get started with the agenda, I want to thank Olivia and her team for doing a great job on Friday night at the opening of SoHo Dufort." She glanced at him and gave him a polite smile. "Katy, you handled the media like a pro. It didn't go unnoticed."

"Thank you, Mr. Dufort," Katy said, sitting up straighter in her seat and shooting Olivia a proud smile.

Olivia was a fantastic leader, and he was impressed with how much effort she was putting into growing her people. Sure, the past week had been a buffer to their attraction, but she'd been focused on both Katy and Thomas's career progression for over a year, and it was paying off.

He knew Olivia well enough to know she wouldn't have delegated to them if they hadn't had the skills to handle it.

She was a professional.

"Okay, let's get started, as I know we have a lot to cover today. Team managers, why don't you kick things off?" He sank back into the chair and let the meeting progress.

As Barbara Little, Dufort brand manager, began her update, Fletcher let his gaze cast around the room. When they arrived at Olivia, she boldly returned his stare.

A mix of emotions stirred in her expression, blazing back at him. Finally, her gaze dropped, and it felt like someone had punched him in his chest.

Fucking hell.

Trina, the internal communications manager, was on her update when she asked him a question. But he missed it.

"Fletcher?" Olivia asked, prodding him.

His eyes darted to hers, then to Trina.

"Could you repeat that?" he asked.

"Will Daniel be in New York for the next quarterly review? We're planning out the monthly Red Couch Executive Interview series that we stream for all staff."

He nodded at Scarlet.

"I'll find out," Scarlet replied, and tapped on her laptop, already messaging Daniel's executive assistant.

"Thanks. That's it from us," Trina said. "Oh, and we have Pink Shirt Day next month, so we'll be working with human resources to communicate the bully-free workplace movement and getting everyone involved."

Olivia uncrossed and crossed her legs under the table and her shoe caught the edge of his pants.

Their eyes met.

Fuck.

"External media," she began, clearing her throat. "Obviously, the big event on Friday went well. We'll be going through all the media coverage and reviewing it early this week. Requests are already pouring in for exclusivity for the next opening, for which we planted the seed." She glanced at him. Coolly. "Well done on that."

He nodded.

"We've had some bad press in Sydney, Australia, after scaffolding collapsed during a routine maintenance. A man broke his leg and collarbone. I'm collaborating closely with the Australian team and supporting them where I can. Good work over there, James."

"Thanks, Olivia. We've had another piece on the breakfast show this morning. Council have been brought in to provide a comment."

Fletcher shook his head. "Slow news week in Australia, is it?"

James laughed. "Yeah, this is such a non-news piece. We need a politician to say something stupid to distract them."

"Which could happen by this afternoon," Olivia laughed.

"You know it, Liv," James said. His Australian accent was strong as he smirked at her.

What the hell?

Were they flirting?

Fletcher glanced at her and a hint of pink hit her cheeks as she slid a layer of that raspberry lip-gloss on and grinned back at James.

Was she doing that on purpose? Had he never noticed the friendship between them?

Well, he did now, and he wasn't happy.

"I sent you that file," Katy said to James and there was more smiling.

Not the same as the smile James had fired to Olivia, though. There was definitely an attraction there.

Not that he could blame the mid-twenties Australian. Olivia was fucking gorgeous.

But she was…

Was?

… not his.

"That's it from Public Relations," Olivia said, turning from him and glancing out at the team.

A few more of the managers shared their updates and then they did a quick round table so the rest of the team could share or ask questions.

"Thanks everyone," Fletcher said. "Have a good week. My door is open if you need anything."

The room slowly cleared out while Olivia stayed seated, tapping and swiping on her tablet. Fletcher walked to the door, closing it when the last person left.

It was something they often did after a team meeting. Unofficially, she was his second in charge, though on the organization chart, all the team managers were at the same level. From time to time, some of the other managers stuck around to chat further about something that had been raised and they wanted to cover without the less senior members of the team present.

Today it was just the two of them.

Fletcher sat.

Olivia pushed her tablet an inch away, leaned back in her chair, and lifted her eyes to his.

"I'm sorry."

"Apology accepted," she replied, crossing her legs and, fucking hell, her skirt slid up her thigh making him swallow.

"Don't ever think your job is at risk. I should never have reacted like that," he added.

"Thank you. I wasn't sure what was wrong." She pulled her hair around her shoulders. "Well, aside from the obvious."

Fletcher tried to ignore the images of him gripping her hair in his hands as he thrust into her.

God, this was going to be hard.

"I'm right, aren't I? It was because of…"

"Us?"

"Yes." He leaned forward. "I am trying very hard to not want you, but I'm struggling. The things I want to say, the things I want to do to you, Olivia. It's not going away."

His eyes dropped to her silk shirt. Her nipples had hardened, begging for his touch.

She swallowed; her eyes dilated.

"I need you to be strong and say no," he added.

"I did, and we can't." She stood. "I should go. Unless there's anything more?"

He shook his head.

"I'll see you this afternoon for our meeting with the sponsorship team."

Fletcher let her leave; her tablet pressed against her chest as if it were a shield, but he knew it was to hide her arousal.

He didn't have that luxury, and he needed to decide what the hell he was going to do about this because the truth was, nothing had been resolved by fucking her.

Absolutely nothing.

CHAPTER FOURTEEN

Olivia returned to her office and let out a long, audible sigh.

Being close to Fletcher was both pleasure and pain. She couldn't imagine not seeing him every day, and yet she was wondering how on earth she could continue on like this.

She couldn't tell him.

He knew, and he was going through his own struggle.

Plus, he could see her reaction. He knew every inch of her body after thoroughly ravishing her. It had been more than that, though, and she wondered if he had been aware. In between the incredible voracious sex, they had lain together talking and giggling like young lovers.

Yet she'd had to draw a line in the sand, eventually.

When he'd asked if they could spend more time together before he left, she had adamantly said no.

Fletcher didn't hide his disappointment.

It would have been so easy to say yes. In some ways, the things in their life that were blocking them from being together were a gift.

Olivia knew Fletcher wasn't a relationship guy. The Playboy of Manhattan wasn't going to play house or stepdad to Sammy. Every second Sunday, when she dropped her daughter off, she felt a pang of envy.

She'd never have that.

Because Simon was a cruel and manipulative man.

He wouldn't control her forever. But that didn't mean she didn't hate him for it.

He was so damn messed up.

So, the fact that she and Fletcher couldn't date because of Dufort policy was beside the point.

He was a billionaire. And a major shareholder in the Dufort Dynasty.

Her employer. And a known playboy.

Once he was done with her, he would throw her away. She'd had enough heartache and disappointment caused by men in her life. She wasn't sure she could survive Fletcher doing that to her. It was better if she said no to him right now.

She had to protect her heart.

She spent the rest of the day with her team, reviewing the press from Friday's event. There were the usual questions about who the Dufort brothers were dating. Of course, Harper and Daniel were a top attraction because of their engagement, and the one photo they'd posed for was plastered everywhere.

Then she came across the next lot.

Which Dufort brother will fall next?

The article featured a photo of Dakota and Fletcher. His arm was around her, his head tipped into her neck, and it was intimate enough that the press was running a lot of press questioning if things were getting serious.

Was he fucking her still?

Obviously, Fletcher had spent the night with Olivia on Friday, but was Dakota the type of woman who was in it for the long haul, allowing him his office romances? Then she'd smile for the cameras when he figured out he needed to marry someone suitable.

She tucked the printed article into her folder and made her way down to his office for the sponsorship meeting.

"Here she is," Fletcher said, pulling out a chair for her.

"My apologies for being late." She wasn't late at all, but as she was the last to arrive, it seemed like the right thing to say. Which made her cringe. She hated saying sorry when it was a lie. Or socially acceptable.

Why did people do it?

Tony Hardy, the sponsorship manager, dived into his proposal for Dufort Hotels to sign up to become a silver level sponsor for a global animal welfare group.

Olivia sat, pulled out her raspberry lip-gloss and absentmindedly lifted it to her mouth. Her gaze rose as she began to apply it and found Fletcher nodding at Tony before slowly turning to her. His smoldering eyes watched her slide the gloss over her lips.

Oh crap.

Moisture pooled in her panties.

How could she say no to a man as she yearned for his touch?

The ache increased as she rubbed her lips together. His green eyes lifted to hers, rich with torment.

He swallowed and looked away.

Remember your heart—he'll break it.

"I believe Dakota Smithers is involved with this charity and I wondered if you could speak with her. See what she knows and dig around?" Tony said.

Olivia pressed her lips together.

Ugh, of course she did.

"I can do that, but I believe she is in the UK this week. Still, I think they have phones over there." Fletcher smirked.

Everyone laughed.

Olivia didn't.

When the meeting was over, they all stood, and Fletcher asked her to stay. He stood, closed the door and returned to stand way too close.

She knew she was overreacting, but that damn photo had wound her up.

"You're angry. Why?" he growled.

She was, but she had no right to be.

"It's none of my business." She packed up her folder and slipped her tablet back inside it.

"Olivia, look at me," he demanded, and her eyes flew to his. "You were with me when we dropped Dakota home on Friday."

How intuitive of him.

She nodded; her lips pressed together.

"You know I've slept with her." He said it as if it was no big deal.

"Of course I do, and like I said, it's none of my business." She lifted her folder and went to turn and leave, but Fletcher blocked her. "Please move."

"For God's sake, Liv. I told you I want to see you more. If that's what you want too, let's find a way."

She couldn't.

It wasn't possible.

He knew that.

"No. No," she said, clenching her teeth. "You know I can't. We can't."

"Then stop snarling at the thought of me with another woman. Because that's what single people do." He growled.

Olivia dropped her folder back on the table and planted her hands on her hips.

"Fine, so you'd be happy for me to take the lead and fly to Australia for the next quarterly update. And sleep with James? I saw you react this morning."

Fletcher's jaw twitched, and he took a step closer.

"Is that what you want?" he asked.

She shrugged.

No.

Not at all. I want you!

"Sure, he's a cute guy. That accent."

Her heart thumped as Fletcher took another step closer and she drew in his musky scent. She held her breath, not letting herself weaken at the sight of his broad chest and flaming eyes, even as they completely dominated her every thought.

"Cute isn't what gets you wet. Cute isn't what makes you spread your thighs and thrash as you beg for more tongue, more cock, more pleasure." Fletcher's voice was low and deep. "I do."

Her mouth fell open.

Holy hell in a handbasket.

"When you realize I'm what you want, let me know." His thumb swept across her lower lip and dipped inside. Her traitorous tongue slipped out to meet it.

She swallowed.

Fletcher's hand slid behind her neck and into her hair.

Oh, thank God, he's going to kiss me.

Then he stepped away.

"I'm not sleeping with her," Fletcher said.

"What?"

"Dakota. That's what you want to know," he said. "I'm not. Or anyone. And until we figure out what this is, I don't want you sleeping with anyone else either."

Her lips parted.

How dare he?

She wanted to tell him he couldn't tell her what to do. That it wasn't his call to make, but every part of her body relaxed, knowing Fletcher Dufort was hers.

At least sexually.

For now.

Even though she knew it couldn't continue.

Her head dipped to hide her smile. But he'd seen it.

"Jesus," Fletcher said. "I can't control myself."

He grabbed his face and dropped his lips to hers with force. She melted into him, and his entire body wrapped around hers.

"God damn raspberry," he groaned as she began to shake with need, their mouths desperate for each other, fingers digging into flesh.

Fletcher ripped his mouth from hers. Their eyes were on fire as they caught their breath.

"Fuck me," he said, shaking his head. "Friday. Bring a bag to the office. You are coming home with me this weekend."

"Fletch—"

"Say no, and I will fucking storm up the steps to your house and make a scene," he said. "You are *mine* this weekend. End of story."

Olivia gasped.

God, she wanted this. Wanted him.

Her panties were a write-off and she'd have to change them. If that wasn't proof she wasn't ready to end this yet, then what was?

Her cheeks were on fire as Fletcher pressed his erection into her body.

"Now unless you want me to discover what color panties you have on, you need to leave right now." He growled.

She clenched her thighs and let out a moan.

"Olivia," he growled again. One last warning.

"Friday," she said in agreement.

Four long days. She had no idea how they were going to get through the week without shagging in the office.

She also didn't know how another weekend together was going to douse these flames. But it was worth a short. All she knew was she desired Fletcher Dufort more than any man in her life.

But. Olivia wasn't stupid. She knew he wasn't the one. This was pure desire.

He was a billionaire, and she was a single mother with a crazy-as-fuck ex-husband. But for one more weekend, she could enjoy the delicious haze of their chemistry as he treated her body like she was a queen.

Then it had to be over.

Forever.

CHAPTER FIFTEEN

Fletcher stood in his penthouse and stared out at the city lights while he nursed a glass of Macallan whiskey.

New York was beautiful at night, and he never tired of the sight. Of course, he had one of the best views but he never took it for granted.

He may have grown up with wealth, but one thing both his parents had done was make sure all three of the boys understood hard work and what it took to create and keep wealth.

They had all started at the ground level of Dufort Hotels, learning the ropes. Not only did it give them a good understanding of what made the business tick, it taught them relationship skills with people from all walks of life.

Not just the rich and famous they rubbed shoulders with. For business or pleasure.

He turned away from the window and let out a sigh. How many God damn days *were* there in a week?

Friday felt like it was a year away, but fortunately it was only one more sleep. He was counting down to his weekend with Olivia like a kid in the lead-up to Christmas.

By damn sleeps.

He couldn't wait to have her here in his home.

Now that they both knew they would be spending more time together, a flirty sexual tension had returned between them. Shared smiles, shooting glances as they walked past each other in the hallway.

Yesterday he had given in and tugged her into the stationery cupboard—which he hadn't known existed till he shoved open the door—and tugged up her skirt as he kissed the life out of her.

He'd lifted her onto a shelf and ripped her panties aside, pressing a finger inside her. Her face had nearly made him cum in his pants. The shock and pleasure of her features as her eyes screamed more had him on his knees the next minute.

Tugging the lace to the side as he slid his tongue through her pussy, sucking on her clit had felt so fucking naughty.

"Fletcher, oh my God," she had cried as an orgasm crashed through her. And she had tasted like heaven.

The next day Fletcher almost danced into the office. Even the board meeting couldn't wipe the smile off his face, although Hunter shot him a look that said *we all know you're fucking Olivia* so that had sobered him somewhat.

Even though they didn't.

No one did.

Hunter thought he knew, and fine, he was right, but he didn't know for sure.

He'd texted Olivia to meet him downstairs after work and instructed Frederick to load her luggage into the car.

When he climbed in, she was sitting in the back seat, scrolling on her phone. Fletcher sat beside her, told Frederick to take them to his place, pressed the privacy button, and then waited for it to slide shut.

Then he pulled her into his arms.

She giggled against his mouth, making him grin.

"I can't kiss you while you're laughing." He held her face.

"I'm so glad you forced me into this," she admitted.

"You make me sound like some sexual deviant kidnapper." He groaned.

"Well, I'm hoping," she teased.

"You will want for nothing, baby," he promised.

Baby?

Since when did he call her baby?

"Anyway, if it's deviant you're after, that's more Hunter's style," he said, settling back in the seat and tucking her into his side. "Actually, forget I said that. Totally inappropriate."

Fuck, he had to remember she was an employee.

"I probably don't need to know that," Olivia said, shaking her head. "So how are we going to ensure we don't get seen together this weekend?"

It was important to them both that didn't happen and while he didn't have a solid plan, with his resources, it wouldn't be difficult.

"Basically, we'll just stay in bed and order in."

Olivia coughed and laughed. "That's your plan. Sex and delivery?"

He nodded slowly.

That wasn't at all what he had planned. Not the entire time, anyway.

Fletcher stared out the window as they drove through Manhattan. He'd never spent a weekend with a woman before—a planned weekend. There had been drunken nights which stretched to the next day, but never more than that.

With Olivia, he wanted to impress her.

He had a feeling his multi-million-dollar penthouse wouldn't do it. She knew he was a very wealthy man, but how she would react to being inside his world was unknown. His personal space would be a different experience, more intimate, than being at the office as colleagues.

Frederick parked, and carried Olivia's bags to the underground elevator, then left them.

Fletcher pressed his thumb to the pad on the wall, and the elevator car arrived. He carefully watched her take it all in and give him a small, unreadable smile.

When the doors opened, he lifted her overnight bag and placed his hand in the small of her back to direct her inside.

"I'm nervous," she finally said, glancing up at him.

He was, too.

"You should be. I'm a bad cook, love eighties music and the place is a mess." He smirked.

"You do not like eighties music." She grinned, and he could tell she was grateful for the comedic break.

Then the doors opened, and Olivia let out a gasp.

Fletcher was proud of his home. It had featured in top decor magazines over the past few years, yet right now all he cared about was Olivia's opinion.

He wanted her to love it and feel comfortable here with him.

"Holy hell, look at the view." She stepped out of the elevator and walked across the vast floor to the windows. "I Googled your penthouse but seeing it in real life... wow."

She had?

Of course she had. That was just the type of thing Olivia would do to prepare. He dropped her bag and joined her at the window.

"This is just stunning." She spun around, then her eyes lifted to his.

His heart beamed with pride. Yet, he wondered, as he gazed down at the beauty before him, if Olivia wasn't the stunning one.

"Daniel's penthouse is amazing, but this is just gorgeous," she said.

Ah yes. She'd seen inside his brother's home a few weeks ago when they'd held a meeting there, after hours, during a media crisis.

"Well, don't tell him you said that, or your job *might* be at risk." Fletcher winked.

After showing her around, he left Olivia to unpack while he poured them a drink. Then he put on some music. He'd had to dig deep to find something from the eighties, but when Olivia came down the stairs, *Call Me,* by Blondie, was playing in the background.

She accepted the glass of wine and his kiss.

Every cell in his body wanted to take her straight to bed, but he also liked the idea of taking a moment to just be together, be able to touch her, hold her, kiss her without having to hide it.

"Are you going to comment?" he asked, smirking.

"No. I'm going to respect your choice of music," she said, stone-faced. "Then change it the moment you step out of the room."

He barked out a laugh, then pressed the remote, changing to a more up-to-date playlist.

"So, what's a normal Friday night at Fletcher Dufort's home look like?"

He tugged her down onto the sofa with him.

"Incredibly unexciting. If I'm not heading to an event, or for a drink with friends or one of my brothers, I'd probably arrive home to a meal which has been prepared for me," he said, admitting to having a chef. There was no point in hiding his wealth. Olivia knew who he was. "Which I'd enjoy with a glass of something."

She reached for his shirt and undid a button, her eyes holding his. "Continue."

"Then I'd open my laptop and turn on the TV. I'd pretend to watch it while working until I can no longer focus."

She shook her head. "You work on a Friday night?"

He shrugged. He worked every day. Being a major shareholder in a multi-billion-dollar global organization wasn't a nine-to-five job.

"Not this Friday." He lifted her fingers to his lips and kissed them slowly. "Tonight, you have my undivided attention."

She smiled warmly and his heart did some weird skipping thing.

"I have a few things planned for us this weekend. Some surprises," Fletcher announced, and her eyes widened.

"Such as?"

"Surprises. Which means you'll just have to wait and see." He held her eyes as he ran his fingers down her arm and watched the hairs on her arms lift while she shivered.

His eyes rose to hers, and the now-familiar flame began to flicker. Perhaps he wouldn't be able to wait.

"Your touch. It's…"

He waited for her answer.

"Addictive."

At the same time as he reached for her, Olivia climbed onto his lap. Their mouths connected and flames began to rage as her warm, wet lips moved in time with his.

God, she felt incredible. He had no idea how he was going to make it through dinner before fucking her.

He didn't want her to feel that was all he wanted from her, because while this may only be something they had for a short time, he needed her to know she was special.

Why?

Because she was Olivia.

That's all he'd been able to work out.

"Let's eat." He released her mouth.

"What do you have?" she said, licking her lips and giving him the sexiest look.

Fletcher let out a groan and tried to focus.

His chef left his meals either in the oven or refrigerator with reheat instructions. Tonight, it was oven baked salmon with green vegetables and charred lemon.

"I hope you like salmon," he said, sliding the meal into the oven.

"Or we're ordering a pizza?"

"Or I'm calling the chef back to make us something else." He turned to find her leaning on the Italian marble and oak center island.

"The luxury of the rich and famous."

"Infamous."

"New York's Playboy," she corrected.

"Does that bother you?" he asked, stepping into her space, and taking the wine out of her hand, dropping it on the island behind her.

"That I'm your latest plaything?"

He frowned. "That's not what this is."

Wasn't it?

If it wasn't, then what was it? The expression on Olivia's face said she was wondering the same thing.

"Is it not?"

"No. Not at all. I don't spend weekends with the women I... date."

Regret crossed her face as she shook her head. "Sorry Fletcher, that was unfair. I guess I should know better, given I work with media. I know half of it is just gossip."

Well, perhaps twenty-five percent.

He wasn't *not* a playboy and made little effort to be discreet. He'd never had a reason to. Fletcher had no intention of ever getting married. He couldn't think of a reason why he'd want to. Dufort Hotels didn't require it of him. There was no financial driver and, frankly, his dick was pretty satisfied with the way things were.

Now, as he held Olivia in his arms, he suddenly cared.

He wasn't ashamed of his healthy sex life, but he did care that she thought he considered her just another one of the women he bedded.

He most definitely did not.

Lying to her, though, was not on the cards.

Fletcher intended to tell her the truth.

"You need to know that most of it *is* true. Some of it is complete garbage." He brushed his thumb over the edge of her eyebrow. "Being with you is different. It's important to me that you know that."

"Don't do that."

"What?"

"Don't you dare let me fall for you, Fletcher Dufort." She shook her head. "We have two days together and then we go back to our lives. Back to being colleagues."

He frowned.

"Jesus. Most women hint, *poorly*, at a marriage proposal after drink two. Yet all you do is push me away."

Olivia tilted her head at him and gave him a sly smile. "Well, consider this your lucky weekend." Then her smile faded. "Anyway, you know why, so let's just keep some boundaries in place."

"Don't be loveable then. Got it." He gave her a quick kiss.

"You don't be adorable." She ran her hand down one of his pecs.

"Not a chance."

"Or sexy."

"Impossible." He grinned, and turned to check on the salmon.

Fletcher could feel her smile on his back. Olivia was right. They were both at risk of feeling more for each other. Even he could admit to that. He knew spending this time with her was not going to dilute how he felt.

Unless she had some really horrible bad habit he'd never noticed.

He smirked to himself as Olivia wandered around the kitchen, finding some plates and cutlery for them.

He loved having her in his home.

Sure, she was sexy as hell, and possibly the most beautiful woman he'd ever seen with all that wild red hair and stunning blue eyes, but there was something comfortable about being with her. It wasn't just that they knew each other. He liked her.

Like, *really* liked her.

Liked talking to her, listening to her, sharing ideas and thoughts with her.

They did it at work, and now that she was in his personal space, Fletcher realized he more than liked having her in it.

He served their meal and they sat at the ten-seater dining table, which he'd had flown in from Italy. They sat down one end, where Olivia lit the candles, and he lowered the main lights creating a moody romantic ambience.

"I love the floor-to-ceiling glass, so you can look out no matter where you are," she said.

"It's why I bought the place," he replied. "We could have sat outside if you wanted." He indicated the large outdoor area. "There are heaters out there."

"No, this is nice."

Her stockinged toes touched his as she dropped her utensils a few minutes later, and their eyes met. Heat rushed through him as he saw the need and hunger in them.

"You're determined to get me into bed, aren't you?" He teased.

"I'm not here to play chess."

"We can."

"I don't know how," she admitted.

"Really?" He was surprised. "Want me to teach you?"

She laughed. "No. Not in the slightest."

"Where did you grow up?" he suddenly asked, realizing how little he knew about her life.

"New York. The Bronx. My dad died when I was twelve, after serving in Iraq, so then Mom had to work a couple of jobs."

"No siblings?"

She shook her head. "No. Just me. Mom helped toward the costs of college for me, and I worked as I studied. We really weren't that close. I mean, we were, but she was just so sad after Dad died and we hardly saw each other. Then I married Simon and a year after Sammy was born, she died of cancer. Brain tumor. It was very sudden."

"I'm sorry."

She gave him a sad smile. "I'm glad she got to meet Sammy. They had a few good months together. Mom and I spent more time together while I was on maternity leave and learning to be a mother than we had since I was a child. It was nice. Sammy was a very easy baby."

Every time he'd met Sammy, she had been a polite and happy little girl.

"Being a parent must be pretty special."

It was something he'd been thinking about recently, especially now Daniel was getting married. It was likely Harper would soon get pregnant. He'd be an uncle.

There would be little Duforts in the world.

He'd never considered what he and his brothers' vow not to marry meant in regard to parenthood.

Now it was on his mind.

Was it because of Daniel and Harper's engagement? It was probably a normal reaction when one of your siblings took the next adult step in life.

Or was it because he was now thirty?

Did he even want to be a father?

There were a lot of questions running through his mind, and whether he wanted to admit it or not, his feelings for Olivia were stirring them up.

What did that mean?

"It's the best and hardest job in the world," she said, finishing her wine.

They sat talking for a little while longer, then he cleared the table.

"That was delicious." Olivia leaned back in her chair. "Thank the chef for me."

"Hey, I paid for it."

"Yeah, how much was it?" she asked.

"No idea, it's just a…" He frowned and turned, then he realized she was teasing him.

"Does all this bother you?" He leaned his hip on the counter, and waved his hand around indicating his house, his wealth. She didn't seem uncomfortable, but he knew it wasn't the way normal people lived.

But it was who he was.

She stood, walking to him. "No. I know who you are, Fletcher Dufort. But it's very different from my life. You've seen my tiny, messy home."

Yes, he had, and he didn't judge her.

Well, maybe her wine.

"New York is expensive. I know what you earn." He cringed. "What I mean is, I know who you are too, Liv. This weekend I want to share all this with you. To enjoy it with you. I've never done that with anyone before. Will you let me?"

She stepped into his arms.

"I'm here, aren't I?"

He nodded, brushing the hair off her face. "Yes."

"Just don't expect me to be one of your socialites. I'm more the Cinderella type who's going to disappear at midnight. Or in our case, Sunday afternoon."

"Night."

"Afternoon. I am a mom. I have kid stuff to prepare for."

He let out a sigh.

Sunday afternoon it was then.

"Then, best we get these clothes off you. I have a hot tub I want to introduce you to."

She grinned.

"Lead the way."

CHAPTER SIXTEEN

Olivia melted into Fletcher's body while the hot, fragrant water bubbled and gurgled around them.

"God, this is incredible." She sighed.

"I'm pretty sure it's about fifty percent nicer with you in it."

She grinned up at his wet, steamy face, knowing hers was the same. He dropped a kiss on her lips, and she realized she'd been expecting it.

Kissing Fletcher was becoming normal.

When had that happened?

She'd meant it when she had warned him not to let her fall for him. After a week of sexual flirty tension in the office—and a seriously delicious orgasm in the stationery cupboard which she'd never forget—and now spending an intimate weekend with him, it was going to be hard.

She just had to remember the stakes.

Her daughter.

Still, there was no way Simon could find her tucked away in this multi-million-dollar penthouse overlooking Manhattan, and she secretly loved that fact.

For once, she had a moment of pleasure to herself, safe from her ex-husband.

Fletcher handed her a flute of champagne, and she took a little sip, staring out at the glittering city lights.

She wondered if wealthy people felt better about their problems when they had views like this?

Probably not, but hers felt a little lighter, and she was going to enjoy it.

Having the most handsome and sexy man she'd ever come across naked in the hot tub with her made it even more incredible.

"You must hate your life," Olivia suddenly spurted out.

"It's horrible." He nodded, dryly. "But why do you say that?"

She sipped her champagne. "I suppose it's an ignorant thing to say. Money doesn't buy happiness."

Fletcher stretched out his legs and lay an arm out along the tub behind her. "No. But it pays for a lot of solutions to problems and things that can bring happiness."

"But don't you think happiness is an inside job?"

"Isn't that a meme?" he asked, giving her an amused frown.

She shrugged. "Doesn't make it less true."

Fletcher looked thoughtful as he swirled and then drank the dark liquid from his crystal tumbler.

"Here's what I think. Happiness is not connected to your bank balance. It can bring pain or joy, but it's what you're thinking and doing with your life every day that dictates your happiness."

Huh.

Olivia was surprised by the depth of his answer. Not that Fletcher was a shallow person. She knew him better than to think that, despite what the tabloids said about him.

"My mother was a rich woman when she was with my father. Still is in some respects. But she was miserable," Fletcher said, taking another sip. "He cheated on her, as you know, many times, and yet she stayed with him, turning a blind eye to it."

"You can only ignore things to a point, though." He continued. "His neglect and disrespect of their marriage slowly ate away at her. She drank a lot and eventually snapped."

Olivia let him continue.

"All the millions and eventually billions did nothing to make her happy. If she had chosen a different path, perhaps she would be happy. Even now she remains a victim to our father."

She frowned. "How?"

"She is a shell of a person. Still drinking, not socializing or dating. Heck she's only fifty-seven. She could marry again and find love."

Olivia smiled, turning into him. "Listen to you, you old romantic."

He gave her a mocking glare, putting his whiskey down.

"Enough talking." He pulled her onto his lap and put her flute beside his glass. "I'll show you how unromantic I am."

She giggled.

"Fletch, we're in a hot tub drinking champagne. Sorry, but that's very romantic."

He mock-growled.

"Stop talking." He flicked his thumb over her nipples. "You will destroy my reputation."

When he lifted her body up and placed his mouth around one of her breasts, all ability to speak left her, so he got his request.

"I'm going to fuck you in this tub and the only thing I want to hear from you is my name screamed," he said, as his fingers slipped inside her. "Oh yes, you are so wet, Liv."

No kidding. They were in a hot tub. But she knew what he meant. And she was.

So hot and wet for him

She'd been in a state of arousal for days. If she wasn't with him, wanting him, she was thinking of him, wishing he was there, touching her.

He pulled her legs around his body, and she grabbed hold of his shoulders. One of her top five parts of his body. As he guided her onto his cock, he continued to swirl his fingers around her clit, and she moaned eagerly.

"Fletch, holy God, that feels… *oh, my God.*"

"I love hearing your moans." He gripped her face, devouring her mouth as she sunk deep over his cock.

She moaned into his mouth as he dominated her tongue and began sliding her up and down his length. She ground into him, pleasuring them both with the stimulation.

"Ride me, Liv, that's it. Fuck my cock."

His eyes, full of heat, held hers as they both thrust their bodies together desperately until his orgasm struck like a bolt of lightning.

"Fletcher," she cried. "Oh, yes, Fletch."

"Fuck, fuck, fuck." He cried, and she felt his hot seed fill her.

Shit.

No condom.

She was on the pill, but it was stupid of them.

As the blur and buzz of their orgasms began to fade, they both locked gazes, and she saw the moment he'd also realized.

"I take the contraceptive pill."

He nodded. "I'm clean. I get tested."

"Same. Well, not that there's been anyone, but whatever."

"No one?" he asked, surprised.

"No. Well, its… no. You know my situation. It's just easier."

She didn't want to talk about this while his cock was still inside her, and fortunately he said no more, just kissed her.

"Good. I like that this body is all mine."

"For two days," she reminded him, and he stared at her a moment, then nodded.

The next morning, they woke after both falling fast asleep following one more incredible orgasm in Fletcher's huge bed.

Olivia stretched and giggled when he pulled her into his arms and kissed her repeatedly on her face, neck, arms and decolletage.

"I'm not your breakfast."

"Oh yes, you are," he replied, and he'd been right. For the next few hours, they devoured each other until they were starving and dehydrated.

When his phone rang while they were eating a late brunch, he put it on speaker.

"Fletcher Dufort."

"It's me, dickhead. You have me programmed into your phone," Daniel said dryly.

"I'm sorry, wrong number." He smirked and Olivia shook her head, laughing silently.

"Are you home? We're a few minutes away and thought we'd pop in," Daniel said, and they could hear Harper in the background saying something.

They both froze, and Fletcher began coughing on his toast. "No."

"No?"

"I'm out at lunch. Brunch. What do you need?" he lied, shaking his head in obvious discomfort at doing so.

"Wedding stuff," Harper called into the phone.

Daniel added, "What she said."

Olivia smiled and lifted her coffee to her lips.

"Can it wait until next weekend?" They both cringed this time. "Or Sunday night?"

There was a short silence.

"Sure. Didn't realize you had plans," Daniel said. "Send me a text on Sunday."

Fletcher pressed a button on the phone after agreeing. He didn't look happy.

"Why don't you go see them? I can go home for a few hours or do a few things," she offered.

Fletcher shook his head.

"No. It's fine. I hate lying to my brother, but if it wasn't for this stupid fucking policy, I wouldn't have to."

She didn't disagree.

Jonathan Dufort's behavior had been disruptive and a risk to the business, and she knew some companies had similar policies, but generally an anti-fraternization policy was a pretty old-fashioned position these days.

"He won't throw it out now Mr. Dufort senior is no longer a majority shareholder?" she asked.

"Not after that business with the senator blackmailing him. It's still pretty fresh."

Olivia nodded slowly.

She'd been included in some of the details around the senator blackmailing a few months ago because of her job. She didn't know everything, but when Daniel had returned from Hawaii, he'd quickly shut it down.

"They can wait. The wedding is months away," he said. "Let's get dressed. I'm taking you out."

Her eyes shot open.

She'd thought they'd spend the weekend shacked up in his penthouse. Going out was a risk.

"Where?"

"Somewhere no one will spot us. Don't worry."

An hour later she was flying through the skies in a helicopter with Fletcher seated beside her, looking illegally hot in a pair of Prada jeans, a pale blue shirt, and the sexiest pair of Versace sunglasses she'd ever seen.

How dare he?

There was no way Fletcher was going to spend the entire weekend locked away with Olivia. While two days wrapped around her body sounded blissful, he'd meant it when he said he wanted to share some of his world with her.

They landed on the helipad of his Southampton home and ran across the tarmac as the blades slowed.

"Wow," she said, losing the battle with her red curls. "I kind of loved that."

He grinned and led her into the house.

"We're not staying for long, but I need to get the keys to the vehicle." He strode through the spacious Victorian-inspired white home.

"Is this your place?" Olivia asked.

"Yes," he said, opening a cupboard in the entrance and pulling out a set of keys. "Let's go."

He was so excited they were here. It had been ages. He couldn't wait to show her around the beachside town.

"Wait. Fletcher. This place is absolutely beautiful." Olivia tugged on his hand, stopping him.

Right.

Yes.

It was.

Fletcher stared at her, then nodded as he glanced around the house. He knew what she was seeing. The wraparound porch with floor-to-ceiling windows offering a breathtaking view of the bay. The open concept living space gave it a modern yet cozy feel—a warmer one than his modern penthouse in Manhattan.

This had been his parents' second home where they had vacationed as kids. When Jonathan had said he was selling it, Fletcher had immediately made him an offer.

In fact, he knew he'd overpaid for it, but didn't care. The value of the house had doubled since then, but it wasn't about that. It was a place that held memories back when the family was happy. At least, as far as he could remember.

Had Jonathan been loyal to their mother then? Is that why?

Fletcher would have been way too young to know the answer, and he couldn't trust his father to be honest. Whatever the truth, it had been a happy time in Fletcher's life.

He rarely came out here, but occasionally Fletcher, Daniel, and Hunter, along with a few friends, would take a weekend and fill the house with whiskey, poker, and laughter.

Daniel had offered to buy half, but Fletcher had declined. No matter where his life took him, he'd keep this house for their family. It was likely that, when Harper had children, she'd want to bring them here. He wanted it to continue to be the Dufort vacation home, no matter what their family looked like.

One day, he might even convince his mother to return.

When they were younger, all three of the boys had ridden their bikes, learned to swim, spent hours on the beach playing and licking ice creams. Then, as they'd gotten older, they had exchanged their bikes for girls and beer.

"We vacationed here when I was growing up. Me, Daniel, and Hunter," he said, quietly. "I've had it redecorated but, yeah, I love this house."

She leaned into him, and his arm went around her as they stared out at the windows at the bay. His eyes dropped to Olivia's face, and he saw a longing he'd never noticed before.

Damn.

He could see her in a home like this, with kids, sipping an iced tea on the porch as the sun went down.

He wanted that for her.

In fact, God damn it, for some reason he wanted to be the one sitting next to her.

Dangerous thinking.

He needed to stop. He had promised her, after all.

"Come on," he said. "You'll love this, I promise you."

He fired up the Model E Tesla and let it warm up before backing it out of the garage. A few minutes later, they roared down the road, the wind in their hair.

"Oh my God, I feel so free," Olivia cried, throwing her arms in the air.

Fletcher grinned.

He pulled into a parking lot near a beach he used to frequent as a young boy, smiling at the food truck. It wasn't the same one, but it still sold ice-creams.

They ordered double scoops and then stepped down onto the white sand. Both of them took their shoes off, swinging them as they walked.

"I can't remember feeling so relaxed."

"As kids, we used to spend hours playing here. At nights building fires, telling stories, getting up to mischief." Fletcher shot her a cheeky smile. "I had my first kiss, just over there." He pointed to a bank with some trees.

"You want to reenact it?" she teased, tugging on his hand.

Fletcher swallowed the last of his cone and licked his fingers. Then he pulled her against him.

"No. I want a new memory with you."

Her teasing smiled faded as their eyes locked. The intensity between them was deepening and he knew he should stop, but no part of him wanted to.

Not for a second.

"Fletch."

"Liv," he said, quietly, deeply. His fingers brushed her red locks over her forehead, and he lowered his lips gently onto hers. Softly they moved, opening, gently swirling their tongues in a familiar and sugary embrace. When they should have separated, they didn't. Her body sinking into his further and his arms tightening around her.

Their passionate kiss continued as the sun beamed down over them. The world simply disappeared.

All he could feel was warmth and Olivia.

She pulled back first, blinking.

"Damn you, Dufort." She stared at his chest.

Fletcher didn't need to ask what was wrong. He could feel it too. Right in his chest. A deep growing feeling that was both new and familiar.

He put his arm around her, kissed her forehead and then walked back up the beach.

Fletcher drove her around, showing her all his favorite childhood spots. Then they returned to the house.

He put the fairy lights on, and she did this little thing where her hand flew to her chest and then made all the noises to tell him she loved it.

It was selfish of him, but before he had to take her back to Manhattan, he wanted to have this moment with her. He poured them a drink and grabbed a throw blanket, leading her out onto the porch swing as the sun began to set.

She snuggled into his arms, and they sat silently watching the sky turn a mix of pinks he had no idea nature was capable of.

"I should be taking photos of this to show Sammy," she said.

"Sometimes even moms need private memories of their own," he said, and she turned her face to his so he could kiss her gently.

"I hate to say this, but you keep upping your romance game, so your reputation is completely destroyed. I may have to blackmail you myself to keep this secret."

He grinned out into the night air, wondering how freaked out she'd be if he told her he'd never done anything like this in his life.

A lot, he imagined.

He'd never brought a woman here. Never even considered it.

Yet here he was with this beautiful woman.

Nothing had ever felt so right as it did now, holding Olivia in his arms. He was beginning to wonder if it wasn't time to start fighting for her.

Because in this moment, he never wanted to let her go.

CHAPTER SEVENTEEN

Olivia chewed the inside of her mouth as they flew the forty minutes back to Manhattan. This wasn't her life, and it certainly wasn't her future, but just for a moment, she had wished it was.

Like really fucking wished it was.

Not the chopper and fancy cars, or even the house on the beach, though it was absolutely stunning and felt like a place she could call home and see Sammy running around and living her best life.

No, it was the moments with Fletcher. Being in his arms. The way he looked at her, feeling desired, adored and... more.

Olivia knew what it was, but she was too scared to let her thoughts go down that dangerous path.

It could never be.

Not while Simon held power over her.

Fletcher reached across, took her hand, and she automatically responded, threading her fingers through his.

When had they become a couple?

Sitting thigh to thigh, flying through the skies as the *chop, chop, chop* sound of the helicopter blades filled the air. That's exactly what it felt like.

He squeezed her hand, and she faced him.

"Is Japanese still your favorite?" he asked through the comms.

She nodded.

"Good."

That sounded promising. It had been an invigorating day out in the sea air. Sushi and a movie would be perfect.

Turned out she was completely wrong.

Frederick dropped them at Columbus Circle, and they walked toward Masa.

Olivia's mouth dropped open.

Not because she thought Fletcher couldn't afford the most expensive restaurant in New York City—he could—but because this was madness.

Any number of people would see them together.

"Fletch! Are you crazy?" She gripped his hand.

She wasn't likely to see anyone she knew in there, because her friends couldn't shell out three hundred dollars for a meal, but he could.

All it would take was one person from the media to photograph them and her entire life would tip upside down.

"Trust me," he said.

She was about to shake her head and rip her hand out of his when the door opened.

"Mr. Dufort. Welcome."

Olivia couldn't believe what she was seeing. Either they had served bad sashimi last week or...

"We have the place to ourselves," Fletcher said, placing his hand on her back and guiding her inside.

Holy shit.

The server led them to a table in the middle of the room lit with candles. The space around them remained darkened and empty, yet they'd cleverly created an intimate feeling, just as it was intended.

Exclusive, important, and highly romantic.

Fletcher ordered a bottle of wine, and then his eyes met hers when the server left.

When they did, she leaned forward a little. "Are you out of your mind?"

He smirked. "Yes. A little bit."

She sat back, and with wide eyes, looked around them and shook her head. "You don't need to impress me."

He lifted a glass of water to his mouth, then placed it back on the table.

"I'm not trying to impress you, Olivia. I'm spoiling you."

Oh.

"This must be costing you..." She stopped. It was completely rude to even mention money, but how could she not?

"I would have paid double. Now stop and just enjoy it."

She chewed her bottom lip in an attempt to stop herself from talking. She wanted to tell him she didn't need any of this, but in truth, it wasn't about her.

It was, but it wasn't.

This was Fletcher's life, and he was putting her in it, in the only way he could. Given their circumstances.

She realized for the first time how much she must mean to him, and it made her heart ache in both a wonderful and sad way.

"You know, I would've been happy to just get takeout from the Sushi Train by the office." She grinned at him as she played with the napkin.

"You say that now, but wait until you've taken your first bite tonight." Fletcher leaned back in his chair.

"I'm sure."

Olivia couldn't help but do a calculation in her head, wondering how much he had paid to have the entire restaurant for the evening.

She'd need to eat an entire week's worth of food to justify this.

Fletcher could buy the business ten times over, but that wasn't the point.

"Are you uncomfortable?" Fletcher asked, narrowing his eyes. "Because that's not what I was aiming for."

Damn.

She hadn't realized she was so transparent.

"No. Maybe. It's just, no one has ever done anything like this for me before. I don't mean rent an entire restaurant, but that, too."

"Then what do you mean?"

She played with the wooden chopsticks, which were intricately engraved, trying to find the words to explain her life.

Her parents had loved her, so it wasn't like she had gone without. But looking back, she wasn't sure they'd had a loving marriage. They'd moved around a lot in the early part of her life because she was an army brat, so she'd never formed best friends like some kids did.

Her father hadn't doted on her or returned home from his missions running across the tarmac with open arms like she'd seen with other families. It was as if he'd kept a part of himself shut down.

Then he died and a part of her mother had died, too.

She never felt neglected, but she most certainly wasn't treated like a princess.

Then, when Olivia had started dating, she'd been attracted to confident men who showed her a lot of attention. What she hadn't realized immediately was the extroverted confidence was hiding a need to control.

She'd left those men without looking back, but it was Simon who had slipped through the cracks.

Gaslighting was slow and extremely harmful. She hadn't seen the signs until they were married a few years. He'd never done anything to make her feel special. Quite the opposite.

He'd made her question her sanity.

It started with little things, like asking if the diet she had started was in fact adding pounds. When she challenged him, saying she hadn't changed anything in her diet, he'd laughed at her and reminded her that she had talked to him about it the month before. He even produced a brochure about Keto.

She'd never seen it in her life.

After a while she had begun questioning herself. Had she changed her eating habits and not realized?

He did the same with their sex life, claiming she didn't find him attractive anymore. She had been exhausted and stressed from the psychological abuse, now she looked back.

She'd told him she was doing the same thing, but he claimed she was going to bed later and wearing different clothing to turn him off.

She'd bought some lacy nighties, and he'd told her she was overreacting to his comment.

Olivia didn't know which way was up from one day to the next.

The subtle abuse was constant.

Fletcher doing this for her, wanting to spoil her, was new. A new experience she didn't know how to accept.

"This is just so kind. So, well, *you*, I guess."

Fletcher reached out and took her hand. "I do have an ulterior motive. Don't make me out to be a saint."

"You know I'm a sure thing."

She laughed and his fingers pressed firmly against hers, their eyes locking. Her smile faded as a million unsaid things passed between them.

The server arrived with their wine and began to pour. Fletcher released her hand.

The moment passed.

Plate after plate of the most exquisite Japanese cuisine was brought out to them in small tasting plates, allowing them to try just about everything on the menu.

It was intimate and fun as they chatted and moaned over the incredible flavors in each dish. Fletcher leaned over with his chopsticks loaded, feeding her.

When she sat back and groaned, her belly full, their plates were cleared.

"I really wish we could walk this food off," she said.

"I could put on some of that eighties music you love when we get home and watch you dance," Fletcher teased.

She laughed at his bad joke.

Home.

Olivia imagined what their life would be like if she lived with him. It wouldn't be just her; it would be Sammy, too. A reality check. A man like Fletcher didn't want some other guy's kid, or any kid, living in his immaculate penthouse.

"What just happened?" he asked.

She looked up. "Nothing. I just remembered a few things I have to do when I get *home* to my place tomorrow."

He let out a small sigh and folded his napkin, placing it on the table. Then stood and held out his hand. She took it and placed a hand on his solid chest.

"Thank you. Thank you for a wonderful day and a wonderful dinner."

He lowered his mouth to hers. "You are welcome."

Their time together was nearly over. She was glad he had let her comment go. Neither of them could change anything, so it was best they just enjoy the rest of their night. Tomorrow she would return to her life and tuck away these precious memories of one of the most magical, romantic days of her life.

CHAPTER EIGHTEEN

The coffee maker hissed quietly as Fletcher scrolled through the news site on his tablet.

He had climbed out of bed after staring at the ceiling for the past hour and a half. Even with Olivia curled into his body, he hadn't been able to stay there, overthinking.

When he heard the click, he poured two mugs and added all the cream and sugar he knew she liked, and a splash of milk in his.

Stirring his, he stared out across the vast space of his penthouse.

What was he going to do?

He was falling for Olivia. It was time to stop ignoring his feelings.

There had been little talk when they arrived home last night. They'd walked into the bedroom, undressed each other and he'd turned on the shower.

With the hot water running over their bodies from all four shower heads, they'd slowly kissed and caressed one another. He'd lifted her, after thumbing her clit, and spread her creamy juices around with the head of his cock. Then slid deep inside her.

Their combined cries as he placed her on the shower bench and thrust in a deliberate and intense motion had been raw and primal.

Emotion had poured from her as her first orgasm tore from her. She hadn't voiced how she felt but he could see it in her eyes.

When they stepped out of the shower and brushed their teeth, she had pulled the towel from him and lowered to her knees. He'd clung with one hand to the sink as his cock slid down her throat, releasing once more.

Then she'd swallowed.

Fucking hell, it had been so goddamn sexy.

Fletcher had carried her to bed, where they'd spent hours running their hands and mouths over each other's bodies, until they couldn't stand it any longer and he'd thrust inside her with the need of a madman.

She'd met his desire move for move. Moan for moan.

When they lay completely spent, he'd opened his mouth to tell her how he felt, unable to keep the words in any longer. She'd placed a finger on his lips and shaken her head.

Moist eyes met his, and he'd pulled her into his arms, tight, not wanting to let go.

She had fallen asleep and eventually Fletcher had drifted off.

This morning, he'd come awake in a rush. His mind worked a million miles an hour.

Olivia was his.

Whatever it took, he was going to find a way to keep her.

After spending the day lazing around the penthouse and dodging yet another call from Daniel, it was time for Olivia to leave.

She walked out of the bedroom with her bag and dropped it by the elevator.

"Let's not do a big emotional goodbye," she said, as he walked over to her. "I'm going to see you tomorrow in the office."

He smiled. "I know. It's not the same though, Liv. Don't pretend it is."

She was being so brave, but he kind of hated it.

He saw the sadness in her eyes and wished she'd say something. Just once.

But then again, she had a big motivator. The risk of losing her daughter was real. He got it. But that didn't mean he was going to accept it.

Not now. Not after what they'd shared.

Whoever this Simon was, Fletcher decided he was going to find a way to deal with him.

He just didn't know how yet.

"I just—"

"Never expected to feel like this?" he asked. "Me neither."

"We can't—"

"I know." He stopped her. Not wanting to hear it.

"So we just carry on." She nodded.

No.

No!

He had no intention of doing that, but until he could present Olivia with a solid plan, he had to keep his thoughts to himself.

He didn't want to panic her.

"We take it day by day." He cupped her chin. How was he going to get through tonight, tomorrow, this week, or any day without those eyes on his, those lips on his? "I would do anything for you, Liv. Anything."

She nodded. "I know."

Her phone beeped.

"Uber is downstairs."

He nodded, hating that he couldn't even see her at home. But if her psycho ex saw them, it would destroy her life.

Asshole.

"Text me when you arrive," Fletch said, kissing her one last time.

When he straightened, she wiped away a tear, and he silently cursed. They stared, both wanting to say more. Then her damn phone beeped again.

Fletcher pressed the elevator button, and it opened. Olivia stepped in. He followed, kissed her again, and then stepped back.

"Bye," she said, lifting her hand in an awkward wave.

"See you tomorrow." He plunged his hands into his pockets.

"Yup."

Then the doors closed.

And his home suddenly felt cold and empty.

CHAPTER NINETEEN

Fuck, fuck, fuck.

Olivia's heels clunked on the tiles as she walked fast to Fletcher's office.

Fuck!

When she arrived, she found Daniel standing in there, arms crossed, one hand on his jaw, chatting to Fletcher.

"Olivia," Fletcher said, looking up at her, far too calm, given the situation. Then again, he didn't yet know what had happened.

She tried to calm herself, but her heart was thumping.

"Hey," she said, forcing a fake smile. "I can come back…"

Please don't ask me to come back.

Daniel raised a brow. "Anything I need to know?"

"What?" she asked, her own brows rising in response. "Oh, no. No media emergency. I was just running late. I'll come back."

She turned to leave, but Fletcher called her back.

Daniel glanced between them for a long moment, and the entire room seemed to freeze as her heart thumped away.

Thump, thump, thump.

"I think we proceed with Los Angeles unless you think Singapore would be the right choice. You have the final vote on this," Fletcher said, standing.

"I'll speak to Hunter and get his thoughts, then let you know." Daniel cast her another strained look.

She smiled casually, holding her folder against her chest.

"I believe Harper is going to contact you this week. Thank you for your kindness to her," Daniel said to her, walking to the door.

She was momentarily thrown.

"Don't be silly. Harper is amazing. I'm happy to help and support her in any way I can," Olivia replied.

He smiled and left them to it.

Her eyes flew to Fletcher's.

"What's happened?" he asked, his voice dark.

He knew.

Fletcher walked to the door and closed it.

"What's wrong?"

Olivia handed him the folded piece of paper. He knew what he was going to find even as he unfolded it.

Shit.

A photograph of them together outside her home the night of the SoHo Dufort opening. It was the moment he took her in his arms before he closed the door.

There was no question he was kissing her.

There was no question it was intimate.

The photograph was taken by a professional photographer and camera. That was obvious.

A reporter.

Simon.

Or someone he had hired.

Who cared who'd taken it—it was obvious it was the asshole.

"What did he say?" Fletcher asked, turning it over, looking for anything more.

There was nothing.

Not a single word.

"Nothing. Fucking nothing," she replied. "Sammy handed it to me when I dropped her to school this morning. It was stapled closed, as you can see from the holes. She said, *'Daddy told me to give you this. Sorry, I forgot last night.'*"

Fucking hell.

The guy was messing with her. Playing mind games.

Seeing Olivia upset like this made him mad.

"Listen to me carefully. I don't want you to react in any way. Don't text him, and don't answer his calls."

She shook her head.

"I can't do that. It's a requirement of shared custody that we communicate."

"He can text you if it's urgent," he snapped and then regretted it.

"You don't understand, Fletcher. He's crazy." Her face was pale and scared.

He wanted to rip the guy's head off for making her suffer like this. Part of him felt guilty for being the cause, but that was bullshit. They had done nothing wrong—company policy aside. This was because Simon was a control freak.

"You need to tell me exactly who he is and who he works for, Olivia. This threat, silent though it is, extends beyond you now. I'm not going to sit around while he threatens you, me, and possibly this company."

As a reporter, he was in a semi-powerful position. Not more powerful than Fletcher was, but unless he knew *who* Simon was, he couldn't do anything.

"I'm sorry. I have to be careful. I don't know how, but he will use this to take Sammy," she said, her breathing erratic.

He pulled her into his arms, and she clung to him.

God damn this asshole.

"I can't see how he can."

"The policy maybe," she said. "If he goes public, Daniel will find out, and I'll be fired. Losing my job will be a good first step to taking Sammy from me. He'll claim all kinds of things. She was home that night you came over and he'll paint the entire thing so I look like a bad mother. They already think I'm a drug user. He's a master manipulator."

He groaned and wiped a hand over his face. It was unlikely it was that simple, but the guy had planted drugs on her, so it was sensible for them to be cautious. Olivia had heightened fear over the situation, but after what she'd been through, he didn't blame her.

This is what bullies did.

Manipulated their victims.

"Daniel won't fire you. I won't let him," he replied, even knowing he couldn't guarantee it. His brother was so emotionally attached to that damn policy, it was going to be a challenge to get him to see sense.

"This is such a mess," she said, and his heart ached for her.

"You know what Liv, fuck it. If this all blows up, you and Sammy can come and live with me."

Her eyes bulged out of her head.

"You don't need a job. I'll... fuck, don't look at me like that. I'm just saying I am not letting him take your daughter. I have resources. I know people in powerful positions."

Olivia shook her head.

"Money doesn't solve everything, Fletcher. I am not letting him get me fired and then becoming dependent on you because you feel responsible."

What?

"That's not what this is. That's not what I'm offering." He took in the aghast look on her face. "Look, calm down—"

Her hand came up. "You did not just say that."

Fuck.

"Sorry. Shit. I'm not dealing with this very well. I'm used to just taking control." He ran a hand through his hair.

If it was up to him, he'd hunt the guy down and destroy him.

"Please don't do anything without speaking to me. I have to go back to work. I've got a meeting in a few minutes," she said. "But we need to… obviously… not do this anymore."

Totally destroying him.

He stared at her, then nodded.

They both knew the weekend they'd shared had been incredible and when they said goodbye last night, it couldn't be the end. At least that was what how Fletcher felt about it. Now Olivia was running scared.

As she walked out the door, he realized she still hadn't given him Simon's surname. It was time he stepped up his game. Simon's days of hurting Olivia were over. The question was, how would he stop the guy?

Fletcher pursed his lips, staring at the empty doorway. Then he made a decision.

He wasn't fucking around with this.

Olivia was too important.

He walked down the hall, and into Daniel's office, knocking once on the open door. "Hey."

Daniel looked up from his laptop and frowned when he saw Fletcher's expression.

"Close the door," his brother said.

CHAPTER TWENTY

"These are not people you fuck with, Fletcher," Daniel said, still frowning at him.

He nodded.

He just wanted their fucking number. If he could tell Daniel everything he would, but the damn policy stopped him.

"I get that. I still want their details."

Several weeks ago, when Daniel had been blackmailed, he'd recruited the help of a private security company. Fletcher didn't know *how* they'd found out the incriminating details that had helped them, and it was better that he didn't.

Some things were best left unsaid.

Simon Whoever-the-hell-he-was needed to be scared out of his wits, and it sounded like this company could do that.

Fletcher could, with a surname, find out where he worked and have him fired, but he figured the guy would see right through that and retaliate. It wouldn't take him long to get another job and there were only so many favors Fletcher could pull without it backfiring.

Plus, being on the back foot with global media companies was not a card he would, or could, play on behalf of the Dufort Hotels.

Not even for Olivia.

This wasn't just *his* company, and it would be playing with fire to risk the family's heritage and livelihood. Especially with someone like Simon, who didn't sound like he played fair.

"You want to tell me what the hell is going on?" Daniel asked, leaning back in his chair.

"No," he replied.

"This is to do with Olivia, isn't it?"

He'd known Daniel would piece things together after seeing her fly into his office. His brother wasn't stupid.

Instead of lying, he was going to be honest.

To a point.

"Yes. I'm helping her with a personal matter," he replied.

Daniel didn't believe him; it was clear by his expression, but for some reason he let it go.

"They're not cheap."

Fletcher let out a laugh. "I think I can afford it."

He was surprised his brother had even mentioned money.

"I'm talking big dollars, Fletch."

Whatever.

"Are you going to give me their details or not?" He stood. "If not, I'll find another solution."

Daniel cursed.

"If this is something I need to know about, or you need my help, you need to fucking ask." He pulled out his phone and swiped the screen.

His phone pinged.

Daniel had airdropped the contact to him via iPhone.

Black Hawke Security.

Fletcher nodded. "Thanks."

"The moment you contact them, consider yourself under surveillance. That's how they work," Daniel said. "A nice little surprise I got at the end."

Jesus.

"I mean it, Fletch. Anything goes south, you come to me immediately."

"Got it." Fletcher left.

He returned to his office with guilt running through his veins. If there was ever a time to confess to Daniel what was going on, it was now. He hated omitting some of the truth for Daniel, but his priority was protecting Olivia.

Until they stopped Simon, it didn't matter what policies Dufort Hotels had. He wasn't going to let Olivia lose her daughter again.

Not because of him, or for any other reason.

But he had to think this through. Recruiting an organization like Black Hawke was a serious move. They didn't exactly work within the usual laws. That's how they got things done.

Fletcher's feelings for Olivia were strong. Stronger than he could ever have imagined possible. It felt like she belonged to him, and it was his duty to protect her.

There were a lot of fucking barriers in their way and unfortunately, his brother, Daniel, was one of them.

He just hoped, at the end of this, their relationship remained intact.

CHAPTER TWENTY-ONE

"Here we go Mr. Dufort. One long black."

"Thank you, Scarlet," Fletcher said, not looking up from his emails.

He had drafted a message to the Black Hawke offices, but it was now Thursday, and he'd still not sent it. He wasn't sure what was holding him back. Perhaps because Simon hadn't done anything except slip a photo to his daughter.

It was hardly illegal, even though it was clearly an unspoken threat.

Fletcher wondered if a conversation with Simon would be beneficial. Olivia wouldn't like it, but sometimes a man-to-man conversation could clear things up.

In other words, he intended to intimidate the guy.

Fletcher was a tall, solidly built, and powerful businessman. Either way he looked at it, the conversation was going to go his way. He'd ensure it did.

Unless the guy was packing.

So, before hiring a bunch of former-marine muscle, it was worth taking a more gentlemanly approach.

And he was using that term *extremely* loosely.

To do that, though, he needed Simon's damn surname.

"Oh, and Olivia called before you arrived," Scarlet said.

His head shot up.

"She's at home with a migraine, so won't be in the office today."

Weird.

Scarlet closed the door behind her. Fletcher leaned back in his chair. Olivia didn't get migraines and in the two years she'd been working for him, she'd only had two sick days.

Both had been to look after Sammy.

Letting out a sigh, Fletcher got stuck into his work, figuring she was stressed with everything going on and just needed a day off. He didn't blame her. For the past few nights, he hadn't slept well. He wanted her back in his bed and in his arms.

By lunchtime, he was feeling more anxious about it, so he tried to call her.

No answer.

By late afternoon and after three more phone calls, he couldn't concentrate. He asked Scarlet to cancel the rest of his meetings and have Frederick bring the car around.

"We're heading to Ms. Olivia's?"

"Yes," he said, deep in thought. "Stop a few houses down," he added, conscious of her concerns. A luxury car parked outside wasn't going to help if Simon was having her watched.

Creepy fucker.

He pulled off his Tom Ford jacket and removed his Prada tie, folding the sleeves of his shirt up to his elbows. The weather was cooler outside, but he was hoping the more casual look would give him an everyday businessman look.

He glanced at his Rolex and decided it could stay. He wasn't leaving that lying around in the car, even with Frederick there.

Not with a value of close to one hundred thousand dollars.

He climbed out and walked past three brownstones until he came to Olivia's place. He ran up the steps and knocked.

And waited.

He heard a small noise.

"Olivia, I know you're in there. Please open up." He shoved his hands into his pockets. It wasn't warm at all out here.

The door slowly opened a few inches and red, swollen eyes met his.

His brows shot upward, and he pushed the door wide open, finding her in a pair of old sweats and a sweatshirt.

"What's wrong? Are you actually sick?"

She looked terrible as she turned from him and walked further into the house.

He followed.

"Olivia. Talk to me."

She turned and wrapped her arms around herself. "No. I'm not sick. I'm sick of my ex!"

He stood, staring. Her hair looked as if she hadn't done anything to it except run her hands through it over and over, causing red spirals to stick out everywhere.

Something was wrong.

"What's happened?" He took a few steps and pulled her into his arms. She collapsed against his chest, and he felt her silent tears as he ran his hands up and down her back. "Please tell me."

Then she stiffened and pulled away.

"He rang me. He's threatening to leak the photo to the media." She sobbed.

Fletcher stared down at her, brushing the hair from her face, but she turned away from him.

"Don't do that," he said, his chest tightening at her physical rejection.

"Fletcher, for goodness' sakes. Don't you understand what this means? For you and for me," she cried. "He's going to leak the photo. Daniel, the board, HR, everyone will know. This is going to be a media disaster. *Manhattan's Playboy involved with his employee.* They'll demand my resignation."

Fuck.

Simon would then have grounds to challenge the custody of their daughter. But it was more than that. It was his job—his responsibility—to protect his company and all their employees. Especially given this was a threat to their reputation, and he was the director of marketing.

"Jesus, when were you going to tell me about this?" he growled. "You can't just take the day off and stay silent like this."

She shot him a look.

"I'm serious, Olivia. Regardless of our affair, this involves Dufort Hotels, and it's your job to raise these things with me."

"Are you fucking joking right now? My *job* is to protect my daughter. First and goddamn foremost."

She was right, but so was he.

She was just too damn scared to see it. Not that he didn't understand her perspective, but Simon had fucked with her mind so much Olivia could only focus on the problem, and not a way out of it.

He ran his hands through his hair.

"I'm pulling rank. You need to tell me who this man is. Who does he work for? Tell me his name."

She nodded angrily.

"Simon Mantle. He works for *New York Today*."

"Is that who he'll leak it to? If so, I'll ring Frank," he said, referring to the editor of the paper.

Olivia ran her hand through her hair, creating more mayhem in the chaos.

"I don't know. He could send it to everyone. Frank will know that and want to jump on it. It's too big a story. *You* are media fodder."

Fletcher leaned against the back of the sofa and cursed. It was absolutely ridiculous that people were this interested in who he was sleeping with. An office romance in an organization with an anti-fraternization policy? Even juicier.

"I'm going to resign," Olivia said. "In fact, consider this my resignation."

What the hell?

He straightened. "No, the hell you aren't. I won't accept it. Let's work this through."

She shook her head.

"What's done is done. I've been thinking about it all day. We got caught. We both knew this was a huge risk and we did it anyway," she said. "I need to meet with my lawyer and prepare a strategy, so I don't lose Sammy."

"I'm not letting you quit. I'll talk to Daniel," he growled.

"We both know how he feels about this." She frowned. "He'll either fire me, or demand I quit. I'm just saving us all the pain."

Fuck, fuck, fuck.

She was right about Daniel's position. Still, the photo hadn't leaked yet and as a majority and equal shareholder, Daniel would have to listen to him.

Olivia stepped up and placed her hand on his arm. "Fletcher. It's over. This. Us. Me. I'm leaving."

No.

No!

His skin felt clammy as he watched *her* comfort *him*. He pulled her into his arms. "No, Liv. Don't do this. This might be the opportunity for us to blow this up and get the policy removed."

She pulled back.

"I don't care about my job. I care about keeping my daughter," she said. "But I'm sorry for all the trouble it's going to cause you."

She was apologizing to him?

"Fuck that, Liv. Stop. I'm not losing you. We can work through this," he snapped.

She took another step away and shook her head.

He glared at her.

"Don't do this." His tone was almost pleading as he closed the gap.

She held up her hand. "No. I need you to go. You should leave. You can't be here. Sammy will be home soon."

So?

He'd met her daughter many times at work events. Fury boiled beneath his skin as he watched her completely shut down and disconnect.

"So that's it? It's over. You're leaving Dufort Hotels and what we had means nothing. Nothing at all?"

She stared at the floor.

"Olivia!" he shouted, and her eyes shot to his, rich with emotion. "Don't tell me last weekend meant nothing to you. I was fucking inside you. I saw the way you looked at me. I could feel you."

Her hand flew to her mouth.

Fletcher stood there, waiting. Fucking waiting for her to come to him. Instead, she shook her head and refused to look at him.

"I'm not asking you to choose between me and Sammy. I'm asking you to trust me to help you. To trust me to protect you." His voice was thick with anger and hurt.

She continued to shake her head as tears poured down her face.

Fletcher squeezed his fists, tensed his entire body to stop from going to her. His every instinct screamed to protect her.

But she wouldn't let him.

"Fletch… I can't."

"I can afford the best lawyers, the best security. I can move you and Sammy in with me. Hell, I would even fucking marry you, to protect you."

Olivia's eyes shot to his, her mouth falling open.

"What?" she gasped.

He took a step toward her.

"I'm falling in love with you, Olivia." He spoke more quietly. "Don't push me away."

When he was a step from pulling her into his arms, she whipped away.

God damn it.

"I can't. I can't do this." She turned her back on him and cried into her hands.

He stood staring at her back, pain lacing through his veins. She had rejected him. He had all but proposed to her. Told her he was in love with her, and she'd turned from him.

He began nodding to himself like a madman, as he looked around the room at everything and nothing.

She didn't love him.

It was clear she felt something, but it wasn't love.

This was why he didn't do relationships. He'd seen the pain in his mother's eyes every day of his childhood. Now here he was, like an idiot, falling for someone who would never love him.

His heart went deathly cold and hardened inside his chest.

"I'll need your resignation in writing." His voice was devoid of any emotion. "Given the circumstances there will be no need to work out your notice period."

She turned, wiping her eyes, and went to speak. He held up a hand and shook his head.

"Goodbye, Olivia."

CHAPTER TWENTY-TWO

Olivia pulled herself together enough to make Sammy dinner and put her to bed.

Then she fell to pieces.

Standing in the shower, she silently sobbed. Afterwards she climbed into bed and buried her face in the pillows and cried until there was nothing left.

Now, as she lay in the dark staring at the ceiling, all she could see was Fletcher's face as he told her he was falling in love with her.

How could he do that to her?

It was so much easier when she thought it was just an office romance. He was a wealthy and powerful man who was completely outside her social circle. They would never work. He didn't want stepchildren. Someone else's kid.

Men like Fletcher married senators' daughters, socialites, Harvard graduates, or successful entrepreneurs. Not a single mom with no assets and savings that wouldn't even pay his mortgage for a day, let alone a week.

He couldn't love her.

She had no idea why he'd said he would marry her. Guilt?

And yet, for a single moment, she had glimpsed what they could have, and hope had flown through her. Then reality slapped her back to the present moment.

Even if Fletcher had thought he meant those things, she couldn't let him.

The next few months were going to be a nightmare. Her lawyer would likely suck all her savings, but if she was lucky, she'd still have her daughter. And nothing mattered more than that.

Even her broken heart.

She rolled over, closing her eyes.

She'd just have to realize there could be no men in her life for at least another twelve years. Simon was an evil, insane human being, but he had her over the coals.

There was nothing she wouldn't do to keep Sammy.

Maybe he would give up this vendetta against her and find someone else to pick on. Or maybe he wouldn't, but until Sammy turned eighteen years old, he could have her taken away.

Not legally.

But he never let the law get in his way.

And she didn't trust he wouldn't do something even worse, like disappear with Sammy. Knowing where he worked, where Emma worked, and having her eyes on both of them as much as they did on her, was beneficial.

It was a nightmare, but it was bearable.

Tears ran down her face as she remembered how she felt sitting on the porch in the Hamptons with Fletcher, feeling as if all was right with the world. She'd felt like she belonged and was cared for.

The look on his face as he fed her the most delicious raw fish and delectable tempura at Masa. Pride, affection, joy.

Perhaps he did love her or was falling in love with her? She was a fool for letting him go, but it wasn't his job to protect them. Sammy was hers to look after and the last thing Olivia needed was to become dependent on a man who had a track record for relationships that spanned no longer than a weekend.

She cringed.

She hated thinking those things about him, but they were true. He was a good man, she knew that, but she needed to be sensible.

She'd made one wrong decision called Simon, and she wasn't going to make another rash decision that would impact Sammy's life.

No. She had to do this herself.

Resigning had been the only option.

Somehow, she'd find another job, even if it was doing something else.

And she'd eventually forget Fletcher Dufort.

CHAPTER TWENTY-THREE

Fletcher swirled the ice around in the bottom of his glass. He should have sent his apologies, but instead he was making bullshit small talk and fake smiling at the *Five Stones* launch.

The premium gin producer had been a supplier of theirs for decades and their events were usually very enjoyable.

Tonight, despite the gin fountain and nearly naked gin ladies, Fletcher wasn't in the mood.

He'd gone over the conversation with Olivia a million times in his head. His emotions were swinging around like a damn pendulum.

One moment his chest hurt, the next he was furious with her. He wanted to call her and demand she admit she loved him.

Then, he gave himself a lecture. She had rejected him. He had to face the truth.

Olivia Miller did not want him.

"Fletcher?" a voice said.

"Huh, sorry?" His eyes refocused on the woman standing beside him.

Lucy Belladonna.

She was the managing director of *Five Stones* and a beautiful woman. Driven, successful, and with a sexy Italian accent. Many times, they had come close to taking things into the bedroom and never had.

He couldn't say why.

Better options? Possibly.

"You look distracted tonight, Fletcher." Her accent was thicker as she laid a red-nail-polished hand on his black Dolce & Gabbana jacket.

Lucy was sharp as a tack, but then again, his usual fun demeanor was nowhere to be seen. She should know he wouldn't discuss personal matters with her.

They were a supplier to Dufort Hotels, not friends.

"Tonight has been a success. I'm sure the new botanical flavors will be popular with guests of our hotels." He tucked a hand in one of his pockets and nodded as a passing waiter took his empty glass and replaced it with a fresh Macallan.

"I see we still can't persuade you away from the dark side." She smirked.

"Not tonight, I'm afraid." He lifted the whiskey to his lips.

Especially if the rumors about gin were true.

Crying juice.

The last thing he needed was more damn emotions. He'd been trying to blot them out, not exaggerate them.

Falling in love was not what he'd expected it to be.

Hell, he'd never even *expected* to fall in love at all.

Maybe on some level he had, but Fletcher thought it would be with a woman who was head over heels with him and he'd kind of love her in return. As in, he'd feel in control and…

Well, he'd always imagined he'd be loved in return.

Unrequited love? No.

Who the fuck would have thought?

The "Playboy of Manhattan" rejected.

Stupid fucking nickname.

"Not to worry. The night is young. I'm sure we can put a smile on your face before the evening is over." She leaned into him.

Fletcher tilted his head.

Lucy was not just flirting but propositioning him.
Perhaps this was what he needed?

Two hours later, his head was spinning. He'd never been an easy drunk, and usually held his liquor well, but he'd been tossing them back.

And he was mixing them.

He couldn't recall the moment he switched to gin, but he remembered Lucy had flung her hands in the air in celebration and the party had switched gears.

The music had pumped louder.

Clothes had begun disappearing.

And so had inhibitions.

Topless women were lounging in the gin fountain and one guy was sitting on the edge with his tie loosening and, yup, nuzzling on a nipple.

Holy shit.

An orgy in New York City.

He stared down at his feet and realized he was dancing. Nope. He didn't dance. But apparently, he was tonight.

Lucy had ditched her suit jacket and her white figure-hugging dress showed off all her best assets as she danced seductively in front of him. It was clear she wasn't wearing any underwear.

Old Fletcher might have lifted her onto a table, shoving up the designer fabric, and licking her pussy. Okay fine, *Drunk Tonight Fletcher* was also thinking that.

Why not... Olivia didn't want him anywhere near her pussy anymore.

And Lucy was gorgeous. There was no doubt about it. Long, dark hair fell to the middle of her back in glossy waves. She was rich, successful, and Italian.

What was not to love?

Not love... fuck love.

Lust.

Desire.

All those safe words.

Fucking love. He wasn't going near that shit again.

He was better off with a Lucy, not an Olivia.

And fuck Olivia and her damn big mouth.

Hot mouth.

Her wet, tight mouth.

Were mouths tight?

Perhaps only if you had a big cock.

It was a good question.

Fuck… he really shouldn't have drunk gin.

His head spun as he reached out for Lucy, and she twirled in his arms. Together they moved in time with the fast beat and sang, throwing their heads back. Then laughed at their terrible voices.

"See. Gin is fun." She laughed and he couldn't help but grin.

A gin grin.

Oh, dear God.

Even his internal jokes were getting bad.

"It's dangerous," he replied, shaking his head.

The song ended, and they moved off the dance floor, past the fountain. Lucy gave it a glance and tugged on his hand.

"No," he replied, laughing. "One photo of us in there and it will be all over the internet."

Damn smartphones.

All it would take was someone to share it on their social media and the mass media would pick it up and run it as a story.

"It may recover your reputation." Lucy winked. "I'm just saying. You have been out of the game a little while."

It was true. He hadn't taken a woman to bed for months before Olivia. He'd been obsessed with her. Look where that had landed him.

Fletcher's eyes blinked as he caught Daniel and Harper saying their goodbyes across the room. Daniel shot him a wave.

Fletcher waved back.

"My reputation is just fine." He leaned closer to Lucy and winked.

Was there some Facebook group they all talked in? Like, who's shagged Fletcher this week?

Ugh. This was why it was important he kept drinking. Life made much more sense when he didn't care.

"Let's try the berry flavor next, shall we?" he proposed.

Lucy leaned in, so their faces were nearly nose to nose. "Oh, no, darling. I think you're ready for the Peach Blush."

His hand landed on her hip to steady her. Then, before he realized what she was doing, Lucy planted her lips on his.

He froze.

To her credit, she didn't give up. Her body melted into his and as an automatic reaction, his arms went around her.

His lips opened, and she slipped inside.

They were kissing.

Suddenly, he felt really fucking sober. He pulled back, not abruptly, to avoid a scene. This was her event, after all.

"I've wanted to do that for a very long time," Lucy said, her eyes shimmering with lust.

So had he.

Pre-Olivia.

"Yes," he replied.

Yes?

What the hell was wrong with him?

A hand ran down his pants and she gripped his cock through the fabric. Then her lips parted.

"Oh. I wouldn't have picked you for a man to let a little booze slow you down." She tilted her head and gave him a superior smirk.

Fletcher adjusted his pants when her hand moved away. He was only semi-hard.

He knew why.

"I'm not usually. Don't take it personally."

In other words, please do. If she was going to be a bitch, he could play that game.

Lucy smiled at him as if she had figured out life's greatest secret. "Oh, my goodness. Fletcher Dufort. You're in love with someone. Who is it?"

The temptation to tell her to mind her own fucking business was on the tip of his tongue. Still, he had to maintain a good relationship with *Five Stones*, so he bullshitted his way out of the conversation.

"No, you're right. I've been on some medication and shouldn't have drunk as much as I did tonight."

She patted his pecs and let her hand sit there. "Well, if there's no one else, then I'm sure I can work you into a much harder state."

Fuck, he had to get away. She might be a beautiful woman, but it was Olivia's eyes he wanted to be gazing into, not Lucy's.

Or anyone's.

It was going to take him a long time to get over Olivia Miller, but he would. One day.

Fucking love.

The next morning, the *New York Times* ran a photo of him and Lucy. It wasn't unexpected. He was photographed every time he went out and with every woman he spoke to.

Still, this one looked sexual. Not posed.

Which was correct.

Except nothing had happened.

Not that a photograph gave you the opportunity to explain yourself. He was used to it, and normally didn't give a shit. Today, though, Fletcher wondered if Olivia had seen it. No, he knew she would have.

Had it upset her?

He was tempted to text her, but his head was pounding.

What would he say, anyway?

Oh hey, I know you don't care, but if you did, I didn't fuck Lucy Belladonna. Hope you aren't fucking anyone either. Love Fletcher.

No more gin.

Ever.

CHAPTER TWENTY-FOUR

"Why are you ignoring my calls?" Daniel said as he walked into Fletcher's office on Monday morning and shut the door.

Firmly.

"I called you five times last night and three already this morning."

Fletcher was, in fact, out of his mind.

He'd told Olivia he loved her last week. He'd nearly fucking proposed to her. And she had rejected him.

Fucking rejected *him*.

He could have proposed to any one of the hundreds of women he'd slept with over the past decade, and they would've said yes before the words had left his lips.

Wasn't that typical of life? The *one* woman he wanted had turned away from him.

Now he had sobered up, everything had come flooding back. He wasn't okay with any of this. Fletcher understood she was scared and didn't blame her. Simon was a psychopath. But why couldn't she see he could fix this?

Fuck the policy.

She wouldn't need this job if she was living with him and married to him. He had all the money and resources she could ever need. It seemed like a practical solution to him. If she were living with him in the penthouse, he'd know she was safe and protected.

In the background, he could work out a way to deal with Simon and even clear her name from those drug charges.

If Simon had lied in a court of law, he could be charged with perjury. There were all kinds of options available to them.

"Fletcher!"

He looked up.

"Do you have anything to say?" Daniel demanded.

"Olivia resigned last week," Fletcher replied, leaning back in his black leather executive chair. He should have told Daniel when it happened, but a part of him hadn't been able to face it.

"Good," Daniel said in an angry tone.

What?

"Why?"

"Because I received this," Daniel said, slamming a sheet of paper on the desk in front of him.

Ah.

That fucking photo again.

He looked up.

"Where did you get this?" He growled, grabbing it.

"It was emailed to me anonymously last night. Minutes before I tried to call you. Five times!" Daniel yelled.

Fletcher ran a hand over his face. He'd turned his phone off yesterday after nearly texting Olivia multiple times. He figured if it was off, by the time he powered it back up and then found her number, it would buy some time to talk himself out of the action.

"I'm going to assume that is Olivia Miller."

Like he had to ask by the obvious red curls on the woman in the photo.

"Of course it's Olivia," Fletcher said, sighing. He was over pretending and hiding his feelings for her. From his brothers, in any case. "Look, her ex is threatening to leak it to the media. He's trying to get full custody of their daughter."

As if that explained everything.

"Well, I'm sorry for Olivia, but that doesn't change the fact you've both breached the anti-fraternization policy. For God's sake, Fletcher. You're the director of marketing and a major shareholder," Daniel growled. "If—or *when*—this leaks, it's going to be a goddamn media nightmare."

Like he needed it spelled out to him.

He raised his brows, irritated.

"They'll be more interested in my single status than our HR policies and you know it," he said loudly, standing. "And it's time we talked about that policy. It's fucking ridiculous and time for it to go."

"It's not going any fucking where," Daniel replied just as loudly.

And there it was.

Daniel was so damn emotionally charged around this topic he couldn't see how outdated it was.

"It was put in place to deal with our father. People have office romances all the damn time. It's not nineteen eighty fucking five anymore."

Daniel's eyes narrowed.

"You know the damage he caused with his philandering ways and now this! We'll be on every goddamn media homepage and social feed around the country!"

And global, if Fletcher's predictions were correct, but he wasn't going to mention it.

"What my cock does is nobody's goddamn business," he spat out, and Daniel let out a long sigh.

"I know this is difficult. Hell, I was in your shoes"—he gave Fletcher a sideways look—"kind of, several weeks ago. It's the price we pay for who we are."

Fletcher knew his brother well. They were a close family. Daniel had a strong sense of justice, so he just had to get him to understand the bigger picture here.

Hunter barged into his office.

"The fuck? I could hear you both yelling down the hall."
Hunter glared at them, closing the door behind him. "What
is going on?"

"This," Daniel said, handing Hunter the photo, then
kicked out a chair for him and they both sat, spreading out
their designer-clad legs.

Then they glared at Fletcher. He sighed and sat back
down.

"I called it weeks ago, and you denied it," Daniel said.

Fletcher ran a hand over his face.

"Nothing had happened back then. I wasn't lying to you.
I wanted her, sure. Hell, I've lusted after her for a long time,
but I knew the rules. Then one day—"

"Enough with the romance novel," Daniel said, shaking
his head.

"Don't be a prick, Daniel," Hunter said, narrowing his
eyes at Fletcher.

"I'm not. I'm being the goddamn CEO. I don't need to
hear the details. What we need is a plan to deal with this if
Olivia's ex leaks the photo."

He was right.

Damn it.

"Who took the photo? And weren't you with Lucy
Belladonna over the weekend?" Hunter asked.

Fletcher chugged back the last of his cold coffee, wishing
he'd ordered two of them, and waved him off with a mutter
of *bullshit media.*

Both his brothers nodded, knowing exactly what he
meant. They were all a constant interest to the mainstream
media and rarely was any of it true.

"Olivia's ex is trying to take her kid from her. Again.
He's done it once, by drugging her and planting drugs in her
home."

Daniel opened his mouth to speak, but Fletcher held up
a hand, halting him.

"She is not a drug user, and I don't know why it didn't come up on the search when we hired her. But it's a moot point, so drop it."

Daniel pressed his lips together, but his gaze darkened as it shot across the desk demanding Fletcher continue.

"The ex, Simon, is a reporter at *New York Today*. He's been watching her every move and saw what was happening between us. He threatened to use the fact she was taking men home to get her daughter from her again."

"Men?" Hunter asked.

Fletcher shook his head.

"She's too scared to fucking breathe, let alone date. He's controlling her."

"Yeah, that's not cool," Daniel said, rubbing the back of his neck. "What an asshole. Simon has now lost his job. I'm ringing Frank."

Shit.

As much as he was happy Daniel was changing his tune, this wasn't the path. He understood that now.

"You don't yet realize how unstable this guy is. Anything we do could mean the difference between Sammy having a mother or not. And living with a damn psychopath."

Daniel cursed.

"I'm not sitting back and letting this asshole drag you and Dufort Hotels through the mud," Daniel said, and stood. "Regardless, I'm adding this to the executive team meeting agenda this week. No surprises. That's how I run this ship. You all know that."

Fletcher shook his head.

"Well, then you need to know I will be demanding a vote to have the anti-fraternization policy removed," he growled.

"Speaking of moot points. Olivia has resigned," Daniel said.

"Well at least you get the girl." Hunter grinned.

Not so much.

"We're… it's over," Fletcher said.

"What do you mean it's over?" Hunter asked. "You both put yourselves in this position for a few nights of hot sex? I mean, I get it, but that doesn't sound like something Olivia would do."

No, it didn't.

"Yeah, well she's trying to sort out her life, so she doesn't lose her daughter. She should never have had to resign." He glared at Daniel.

"Hey, the policy was a unanimous decision which *you* voted for when we put it in place."

"Nearly ten years ago, for fuck's sake," he snapped back.

"Can't you help her with Sammy?" Hunter asked.

They'd all met the cute little curly-haired Olivia mini-me at work events where employees brought spouses and children along. She was a standout kid with a bubbly personality, so it was hard to not know who she was. Plus, Olivia worked closely with the executive team, so Sammy had chatted with them all many times.

As much as a little kid did.

He shook his head.

"She doesn't want me, or my help," Fletcher replied, feeling pathetic as he tapped his pen on the desk, frustrated.

The room went silent.

He looked up and found his two brothers staring at each other. Both sported surprised expressions.

Finally, Hunter turned to him. "Jesus, Fletcher. You're in love with her?"

He let out a groan.

"Yes." He nodded, knowing there was no way he could hide it from his brothers. They all knew each other far too well. "Now get the fuck out of my office. I have work to do."

Fletcher spent a few hours with Katy after announcing to the wider team Olivia was on extended personal leave. He'd confided the truth to Katy, asking her to keep it confidential, and preparing her for the potential media storm.

Should it happen.

In a nutshell, their response would be *no comment.*

All they had was one photo of him and Olivia together. Sure, it was clear they were embracing and kissing, but unless one of them spoke, there was no story. It was simply tabloid gossip.

Trying to defend yourself, in his experience, only added fuel to the fire.

He was confident Olivia would do the same.

He spent the rest of the day catching up on emails and preparing for the leadership team meeting, where he was determined to have the anti-fraternization policy overturned.

Because Olivia didn't deserve to have her job taken from her, which, despite her resignation, was what had happened here.

She'd thought it was that or get fired.

Plus, he wanted her in his life in some capacity.

Even if it was only as his PR manager.

CHAPTER TWENTY-FIVE

Olivia placed the coffee in front of Addison and sat on the stool next to her while the girls played in the living room. It was Simon's week to have her, but he had a work event that night, so she had picked Sammy up after school.

"I can't believe it. I mean, I can, but I still can't," Addison said, shaking her head.

Olivia had needed someone to talk to, so had confided in her friend. The upset had been too much for her to take alone.

It had been days since she'd seen Fletcher, and then the photo of him with Lucy Belladonna had been like a knife through her heart.

The truth was, she was brokenhearted.

"I know. It was stupid of both of us. I should have said no."

"Well, Fletcher Dufort is..." Addison lowered her voice. "Hot as hell. I'm not surprised."

Olivia let a small, sad smile hit her lips. "Yeah, he is. But he's a nice guy too."

It wasn't like he was a stranger she'd bumped into at a bar. She knew Fletcher well after working together for two years. And now, after all the intimate time they had spent together she really knew him. Heck, he'd taken her to the Hamptons, to his family home.

"And richer than God," Addison said. "Sienna, feet off the sofa!"

Sammy came running over and Olivia handed her the juice boxes she had meant to take over to the girls. Her mind wasn't focused. At any point Simon could leak the photo and their lives would change.

"Well, it's kind of romantic in a way," Addison said, lifting her coffee to her lips.

"How is that?" she asked.

"You really don't get it?" When she shook her head, her friend continued. "It's like Cinderella. Harry and Meghan. A real-life fairy tale."

Olivia choked on her coffee and began coughing. "It's nothing like that at all. *And* Meghan was a wealthy and award-winning actress well before she met Prince Harry."

Addison shrugged. "Well, that's how the media will see it if the story breaks. Everyday New York gal meets her billionaire prince and…"

"And? We're going to live happily ever after?" Olivia scoffed, annoyed.

Why did everyone think that? Even Addison, who knew how dangerous Simon was.

"What did Fletcher say about the photo?"

She glanced away.

"I resigned."

"What?" Addison whisper-yelled, obviously so she wouldn't freak the girls out. Their little inquisitive heads popped up, anyway. "What? Why?" she repeated in a normal tone.

"Because when they find out, I would have been fired for breaching the company policy, so this way, it's not on my record. It could save me if Simon does try to bring an incompetence suit against me." She chewed her bottom lip. "But I do need a new job, and fast."

"And he didn't try to stop you?"

"Yes, of course he did. He even…"

"Even?"

Her eyes filled.

"Honey, what did he do?" Addison asked, her hand on Olivia's arm.

"He told me he loved me... and suggested we get married." She whispered her confession, a tear spilling down her face.

"Oh, my God," Addison said, her hand flying to her chest. "You have to marry him."

Olivia let out a watery laugh.

"Don't be crazy. You know how insane Simon is. If I dared marry anyone, let alone the Manhattan Playboy Fletcher Dufort, it would set him on a path of destruction that's not even worth contemplating."

Addison shook her head.

"Look, he got away with lying and drugging you once. It doesn't mean he'll do it again. Perhaps you need to speak to the cops? Or a detective? Or, I don't know... but he cannot keep you locked in fear like this. It's unhealthy."

Olivia stared across the room at her daughter, who was playing with a Barbie doll and half watching a show on the Disney channel. Sienna was changing her doll into a new outfit.

Such innocence. As it should be.

She knew she was hyper-alert to her ex-husband and probably overly concerned. That was how victims lived.

The first thought she had every morning was worrying about what he might do. She would try to find anything she may have done that could give Simon cause or an opportunity to mess with her.

To take Sammy from her.

"I know. But this is my life. I married him and these are the consequences," she said.

"Do you love Fletcher?" her friend asked.

She dropped her face and began slowly shaking her head.

"It doesn't matter. Even if I did, I can't allow myself to go down that path or feel anything," she replied.

Addison shook her head. "You're just scared and trying to do this on your own. I think you should talk to him. Not Simon. Fletcher."

Olivia couldn't do that.

It had been nearly a week, and she missed him like crazy. If she heard his voice, she'd break. In any case, it was unlikely he would want to speak to her after the way they had ended things.

She had hurt him, and his goodbye had cut through her heart like a knife.

She had to let him go.

CHAPTER TWENTY-SIX

Fletcher walked into the Wednesday executive team meeting with determination pulsing in his veins.

Daniel walked in with an equally determined look on his face.

Ah, this was going to be fun.

Hunter sat down and shot him a look as the rest of the executive team piled into the room.

Had he approached each of the team members over the past twenty-four hours? Yes.

Had Daniel done the same thing?

Yes.

That's how this game was played.

Fletcher, however, was confident most of the team saw things his way, but one could never be sure until the game ended.

"Right, let's get started," Daniel said, nodding to Selena, his executive assistant, to pull up the agenda on the screen. "As you all know," he said, shooting Fletcher a look, "we have a vote pending at the end of the meeting."

He slowly raised his brows and held Daniel's stare.

Don't try to intimidate me, brother.

He may be the eldest of the Dufort brothers and in the CEO role, but that did not make him any more intimidating than either him or Hunter. The CEO role was a position, a job that required Daniel to make decisions and direct the strategy of the organization. When it came to policy and broader decisions, those were dictated by the entire executive team or the board.

Or both.

That was the reality of a listed public company.

Had Daniel owned the company outright, it would be a different story.

But he did not.

The meeting continued as usual, covering the sales update from Hunter, financials, human resources, and marketing. Fletcher shared his update and then it was time to discuss the policy.

"Anything else before we dive into the last point?" Daniel asked.

Everyone shook their heads, and the tension increased throughout the room.

"Good, then I think we can get straight to the point," Fletcher jumped in. "As my brother pointed out, you all know what this is about." He darted a look in Daniel's direction. "It's been ten years since we voted in the Anti-Fraternization Policy for employees and today, I am asking the group to revisit that."

A few heads nodded, while others took awkward sips of water.

Everyone was well aware this was a confrontational subject between the brothers.

"I've done some research and in the United States, only three percent of organizations still have this type of policy in place."

One or two people nodded slowly.

"That's correct," said Miranda, director of human resources. "I spoke to a few of my industry colleagues, and it appears there is little appetite for it with the increase of Millennials and Gen Y in the workplace."

A few members of the team wrote that down.

"That may be so, but they don't have the history we have at Dufort," Daniel said. "I think we all need to look at the elephant in the room and realize from an employment reputation Dufort has struggled."

Fletcher didn't disagree… if it had been ten or even five years ago.

Which it wasn't.

"Those days have passed, Dan," Hunter said. "Johnathan is no longer working in the business."

Daniel shook his head.

"How long will that reputation hang around? Surely Dufort Senior hasn't caused any trouble for a while now." Tony, the director of finance, spoke up.

He'd been with Dufort Hotels a long time, so if anyone had an opinion outside the brothers, his would be valuable.

"Do I need to remind everyone what I went through a few months ago? Christ," Daniel said, shaking his head.

"Come on, Daniel, that was an anomaly and nothing to do with the purpose of this policy," Fletcher snapped.

Angry eyes met his.

"Pray tell how you come to that conclusion, Fletcher. You know more than anyone in this room the details of the blackmail. It was because of the sexual involvement our father had with a previous employee," Daniel snapped.

Fletcher shook his head.

"Decades ago!" he growled. "Decades, Daniel. And our father was a scoundrel, to put it bluntly. Its 2022."

He glanced at the director of HR. "Miranda, with the *Me Too* movement, and our current culture, would you confidently say if there was any sexual harassment happening inside Dufort Hotels, that staff would speak up?"

She frowned. "Yes and no. It's still a gray area."

Daniel lifted a brow as if he'd proven a point.

"However, this policy," she said, lifting up the printed copy she had brought with her, "makes no difference. It's a cultural behavior of our time. What we're ultimately creating by keeping it in place is an environment where people have to sneak around *or* possibly not speak up about harassment because it could backfire, and they might risk losing their job."

Well, he hadn't thought of that. One look at Daniel's face and he could see his brother hadn't, either.

"Especially if its someone senior. Which, in most cases, it is," Miranda added.

He didn't want to push the knife in further, but now that they were here, he asked his final question.

"And Miranda, what do our recent surveys show in regard to employment brand reputation?"

He knew the answer.

She flipped through some pages and pushed her glasses up on her nose. "Eighty-five percent. Which," she said, glancing up at him and Daniel, "is excellent."

Daniel let out a long sigh and tapped his pen rapidly on his folder.

"Okay, does anyone have any questions before we vote?"

"If we vote this out," Hunter asked, "what support will we put in place to ensure those who *are* being harassed have a path to go down, so that they feel safe?"

"And one that can't be taken advantage of by upset employees," Brent, their corporate lawyer, added.

"Excellent points," Daniel said.

"I've got some ideas on that, and information from colleagues in other organizations. I can work with Brent to draft new policies and procedures to ensure staff are protected," Miranda said.

"If we vote it out," Daniel added.

Fletcher pressed his lips together to hold back his smile. The policy was dead. They all knew it.

Daniel grimaced and let out another long sigh.

"Raise your hand if you agree the Anti-Fraternization Policy should remain."

Daniel and Brent lifted their hands.

"Jesus," Daniel muttered. "And raise your hand if you agree it should be removed and replaced with the new yet-to-be-drafted policies."

The rest of the team raised their hands.

Daniel turned to look at Fletcher and nod. "Fletcher, you have your wish. After today's discussion, I have heard sound reason and while I still believe the policy has some value, I respect your votes. Miranda, make fast work of the new policy. Let's announce this on Monday with the new framework."

Fletcher nodded.

"I don't want anyone employed here feeling at risk, or that they can act inappropriately," Daniel added.

"But to be clear, relationships can take place between employees and Dufort Hotels has no say in the matter unless their behavior or performance is inappropriate or affects their work," Fletcher clarified.

Sometimes it helped to just spell things out clearly.

Daniel closed his laptop and nodded. "No shagging in the goddamn hallways."

Hunter snorted.

Fletcher stood as Daniel walked toward him. They shook hands.

"Well played. And well earned." Then his brother added more quietly. "Go get your girl."

CHAPTER TWENTY-SEVEN

Fletcher glanced at his watch for the hundredth time. He knew Sammy was at her father's house and had been expecting Olivia to be home.

But she wasn't.

It was probably insane to be waiting outside her house, but he hadn't wanted to text her. He'd spent the entire night thinking about how to approach this conversation with her after the meeting yesterday and was no closer to an answer.

So, he was winging it.

Even though she could reject him again.

This time, he was parked outside her apartment and Frederick had the evening off. She'd spot his car if she was looking, but he didn't care.

He wanted her to listen to what he said, just for a few minutes.

A cab pulled up and Olivia climbed out.

God, she was a sight for sore eyes.

She wore a pair of tight blue jeans, tan boots, and a long coat. Her hair was half hidden under a woolen hat.

The cab drove off, and she began to walk up the stairs to her brownstone when she paused, before turning to stare at him leaning against his car.

Fletcher took a few steps and stopped before her. Her eyes were full of emotion, and it took a lot of effort to not reach out and run his fingers down her cheek.

He smiled. It was a small, warm smile which he hoped would let her know he was here to help, not upset her.

She returned his smile, then turned and walked up the rest of the steps.

He followed.

Her keys jingled in her shaking hands for what felt like hours as he stood behind her, dying to touch the back of her neck. Then finally they were inside, and the door closed.

She pulled off her coat and hat, hung it up and then took his.

Then she turned.

"Hi," she said softly.

"Liv," he said thickly, and pulled her into his arms, resting his forehead on hers, his eyes closed as he breathed her in. "God, I miss you."

When he released her, they walked further into the house, and she pulled a couple of bottles of water out of the fridge.

"I've drunk too much this past week," she said. "Is water okay?"

He smiled. "Me too. And yes."

He took the bottle from her, realizing that winging it may not have been the best strategy. He still didn't have any answers, but he couldn't stay away.

And, whether Olivia loved him or not, he couldn't sit back and let Simon hurt her.

They sat at the small dining table, and it was all kinds of awkward. She smiled at him and sipped her water.

He cut straight to the chase.

"The anti-fraternization policy is dead. It's been removed."

Her mouth fell open. "How?"

"I fought for it. It's outdated—we both know that. And, as it turns out, many of the executive team felt the same. It was a bit of a battle, but in the end, the majority voted it out."

"Is Daniel pissed?" she asked.

He smirked. "A little. But he's not a dictator, so he accepted the vote."

She pressed her lips together and smiled. "I'm glad."

"So the photo remains out of the public eye." He said, leading the conversation to his next point.

Olivia let out a sigh. "For now."

"What did he say when you dropped Sammy off?"

"Nothing. He just gave me a smarmy grin. He's trying to control me as usual."

His blood began to boil. How did she put up with this day after day? Fletcher couldn't sit by and watch this man harass and manipulate the woman he loved.

He just wouldn't.

"He *does* control you," he said, gritting his teeth.

And him.

Whether Olivia realized it or not, by association Simon was also controlling Fletcher. That was not fucking okay.

But it wouldn't be like that for much longer.

Olivia shot him a dark look. "Thanks, Fletcher. Do you think I don't know that?"

And this is why 'winging it' was a terrible fucking strategy.

"I'm sorry." He threaded his fingers through his hair. "I'm just frustrated. I want you in my life, Olivia. I can't stand not seeing you. I want you to come back to work, at the very least."

She shook her head.

"It's too dangerous. Perhaps he hasn't leaked the photo yet because he knows I've quit. Whether it's you and me, or the job. I don't know."

He reached for her hand and, thank God, she let him.

"Don't you see? It doesn't matter. The policy is gone. Even if he *does* leak it, you don't have to resign. Your job is not at risk."

She hung her head and stared at the table. "He'll find something else. He's not going to stop."

Fletcher stood and pulled her to her feet. He needed her to be strong and feel safe. He was searching for the words to reassure her but getting through her barriers and independence was nearly impossible.

Damn it.

"No. He won't. He won't stop now, *or* if you have another job, or meet another man. He'll never stop. You have to decide to not let him control you. Let me help you."

His jaw clenched as the words fell from his lips.

Olivia, in the arms of another man, was unthinkable.

He wouldn't allow it.

She was his.

"Tell me you don't feel something for me. Tell me directly right now if you don't, Liv. I need to hear it if you truly don't."

Tears filled her eyes.

"Say it."

She swallowed.

"Olivia Miller, tell me you are not falling in love with me."

"Of course I have feelings for you, God damn it." She tried to pull away from him, but he held her arms. Her eyes shot to his. "I'm trying to protect my heart as well as my daughter."

A burst of hope flashed through him.

Her heart.

She did feel as he did.

"You don't understand what it means to be a parent, Fletch. She is my flesh and blood. I would do anything, and I mean anything, to protect her."

He nodded.

He may not be a father, but he loved his family and felt the same about his brothers. No, it wasn't the same as having a child, but he understood loyalty and doing anything for those he loved.

Fletcher loved her even more for being a protective momma bear. He just wished she would let him in so he could help.

"You have good reason to be afraid, Liv. I get it. But I promise whatever he throws at us, I will protect you."

Tears fell down her face.

"Do you really love me?" she asked.

"Yes."

She swallowed as more tears fell.

"I love you more every single day," he said, and when her face softened, he dropped his lips to hers. She leaned into him, and he wrapped his arms around her, kissing her deeply.

"Come back to work. Even if you work remotely for a little while."

"What did you tell everyone?" she asked.

"I said you were on personal leave. Only the executive team knows, and Katy in case anything came out in the media. They all know I am offering you your job back," he said. "My feelings aside, you are an exceptional PR manager and Dufort Hotels wants you back. Not just Fletcher Dufort."

She smirked and sniffed, rubbing her nose.

"What?"

"I leave you alone for one week and you start talking in the third person," Olivia teased, wiping her tears.

He grinned. "See. I need you."

She stared at him for a long moment, and he gave her the space she needed.

"Okay."

"Okay?" Hope soared through the roof now. "Okay, what?"

"I will come back, but I'll work remotely for a week just to let the dust settle."

Fletcher nodded.

"You have your laptop still, so I'll let the team know." He hadn't bothered asking her to return the Dufort property because he was hoping she would come back or at least come back to him.

Which left one last discussion.

He cupped her face and slightly raised his brows.

"Olivia—"

"I'm scared, Fletcher. He's intimidated by you, I suspect, and honestly, long term, am I really someone you want to be with? I'm a divorced woman with a kid. A single mom."

As he shook his head and frowned at her, she continued.

"Think about it. You're a successful businessman. A billionaire. You date models, socialites, senators' daughters. I mean, you've probably dated royalty."

Well, only once, but he wasn't going to share that minor detail at this moment.

"I've never been happier than when we were walking along the beach in the Hamptons," he said. "That entire weekend, I shared more of who I am with you than with any other woman, except obviously my mother. I don't care about your bank balance or your social status. I like you. I like talking to you, laughing with you, eating ice-cream with you. I'll even drink your horrible wine."

She let out a little laugh.

"Scrap that last bit."

She smiled up at him with glittering eyes. "That was a wonderful weekend."

He brushed the hair from her forehead.

"Maybe I *am* turning into a romantic, but I think it would be stupid for us to throw this away. We have something. I know you feel it. I know you're scared to say it and that's okay for now. Hell, I swore I'd never marry after watching my parents' relationship, but Liv, I would do anything to be with you."

"I'm not asking you to marry me, Fletch."

No, but he kind of wanted to.

He didn't want to freak her out. Tonight was about getting her to trust him again and know she could rely on him to protect her.

His own insecurities could just wait a fucking moment.

"I'm not. When I do ask, you will know. And it won't be standing in the middle of your house," he said firmly.

A blush hit her cheeks and bounced directly into his heart.

God, he really did love her.

"Spend the weekend with me." He ran his hand down her arm and landed on her hip. "I need to feel you in my arms and know you're safe. And mine."

Her eyes sparkled with tears, but now there was a touch of happiness in them. She was letting her guard down.

"All right. But it's probably best if we go to your place. Or hide your car."

Which they both knew was an impossibility in New York City. There was nowhere to park near her house. He had his own private parking spot under his building.

"Let's go to mine."

A few hours later, Fletcher lay with Olivia in his arms while she slept soundly. He turned his head and stared out at the moonlight pouring into his bedroom.

They hadn't stopped to close the blinds or turn on a light after walking through the door. He'd taken her bags, dropped them on the floor then pulled her into his arms.

God, it was incredible to have her back where she belonged.

He truly believed that.

Olivia Miller was his.

Fletcher wanted her here every damn day of his life. That meant Sammy too, and that would mean building a relationship with the little girl. It would take time—heck, right now she called him Mr. Dufort.

Well, in truth she called him Fletcher in secret, but her mother didn't know that. It was their private little joke when she came to staff functions.

Sammy was a cute kid. He liked her. But could he be a stepfather?

He'd probably be a better role model than her narcissistic, controlling father. Not that he was qualified to label the guy, but it was kind of obvious.

He tucked his arm under his head. He'd do whatever it took to be the best stepfather to Sammy and protect them both.

The next morning he had showered and dressed, and Olivia still hadn't stirred.

"Hey, sleeping beauty," he said, sitting on the side of the bed kissing her forehead.

"Hey," she said, opening her eyes then bolting upright, nearly smashing heads with him.

"Whoa," he laughed.

"What time is it?" she asked, rubbing her eyes. The sheets fell to her lap, and he tried really hard not to cup her breast.

And failed.

"Eight thirty. I've got a wedding meeting with Daniel and Harper in thirty minutes. I better go to this one." He smirked. "I'll be home after lunch."

She moaned into his touch.

"I better go, or I'll be late." He kissed her lips and then decided life was too short not to enjoy what was in front of him.

He leaned down and suckled on her nipple as she fell back onto the pillows. Her fingers slipped through his hair.

"Oh, God, Fletch." She groaned as his tongue circled the pink globe.

Shit.

He tugged the sheet down and pushed her legs apart.

He was going to be late.

CHAPTER TWENTY-EIGHT

On Wednesday, Olivia walked into the Dufort Hotel offices. It had been nearly two weeks since she had agreed to come back.

She'd stayed at Fletchers all weekend, making love to him and snuggling on the couch. Aside from Fletcher going to see Harper and Daniel, neither of them left the house until she had to collect Sammy.

Which she did on the way home.

Simon had given her bags a raised brow glance when he walked Sammy to the cab and kissed her goodbye.

Watching her daughter throw her arms around her father, she wished, not for the first time, that he wasn't such a dick.

But he was.

A dangerous one.

"Good weekend?" he asked, as Sammy got herself buckled in.

"Goodbye, Simon. See you on Sunday." She pulled the door closed. He grabbed and half-opened it. Gave her a long look and then closed it.

Ugh.

Fletcher was right. Simon was controlling her. She'd had enough. He wasn't above the law, and while he had gotten away with drugging her and lying last time, she would never let him into her house to do the same thing again.

Olivia usually checked Sammy's bags when she got home, too. The weekend she hadn't spotted the photo was because she had been all loved up after such a romantic weekend with Fletch.

A mistake she wouldn't make again.

She grabbed Sammy's bags while the cab drove them home, checking them but lying to Sammy about what she was doing, as she did every week.

"Any homework?"

"All done, Mom," Sammy said, rolling her eyes.

Olivia smiled. At some point, she had to stop doing this. She didn't want her daughter growing up thinking she didn't trust her. Every damn thing a parent did impacted their child's psyche. Having a narcissistic father was enough for her little girl.

"I don't need to check, do I? You are so good."

"Well, I do need a costume…"

"What?" she had asked, her eyes widening.

"Just kidding, Mom." Sammy had giggled while Olivia tickled her.

Trusting Fletcher, she thought as she walked through the office, was difficult, but she was trying. When she was with him, they lived in their own private sexy bubble.

Sooner or later she would need to introduce him to Sammy as her boyfriend, but she needed to be sure Fletcher truly loved her and it wasn't just a passing phase. Yes, they had lusted after each other for a long time, but he had never been in a long-term relationship. Throw a child into the mix and she did wonder if the reality might be a little too much for him.

Right now she needed to focus on work.

Fletcher had said Katy was aware of what had transpired. She trusted her, as Fletcher had, and he had done the right thing. Dufort Hotels had needed to be prepared for a media crisis had it hit.

Fortunately, it hadn't.

Yet.

After a few meetings with her team, she made her way to Fletcher's office for their weekly catch up.

She closed the door behind her as he looked up.

"How's the first day back going?" he asked, standing to greet her.

She dropped her things on the table and let him pull her into his arms. "Wow, so we can do this now?"

Fletcher laughed. "I'm pretty sure we're not supposed to be making out in the hallways now the policy is gone, but yes, we can do this."

His lips found hers and their kiss went from soft to deep in seconds. It was always that way with them.

"Although, I'd really love to lift you onto my desk and spread your legs, Ms. Miller."

Jesus.

Heat flared through her body in a rush.

"Fletch," she moaned.

His hand ran down the side of her body and found the edge of her skirt.

"You want that, don't you?"

She wanted to say no, but God help her.

"Come here." He tugged her to his desk and did exactly as he had said. Lifting her onto his desk, pushing aside a few things.

"Oh my God, what if someone comes in?" she gasped.

"What if?" he smirked, tugging her panties down.

"Fletcher."

His hands spread her legs, causing her skirt to move up, exposing her.

"Never do I tire of this view." He slid his fingers through her. "Holy hell, you are so wet already."

His eyes shot to hers. Then he stormed to his door and locked it. When he returned, he was undoing his pants.

Oh my God, they were really doing this.

"Lay back on your elbows," he ordered her, his fingers returning to her flesh as his other hand stroked his cock.

She licked her lips and let out a moan as he found her clit.

"Fuck, I want to be in you and taste you," Fletcher said, leaning down and lapping his tongue in one long lick across her pussy.

"Oh, God, Jesus, God," she said irrationally, her body trembling.

"That's it, baby. Come on my mouth, if you are ready." His tongue worked her clit and his fingers plunged into her, and her body erupted.

Pressing her lips together, she barely kept her cry to a normal level, groaning and moaning out her pleasure. When her eyes opened, Fletcher was standing, pressing his cock at her entrance.

He leaned over her and thrust inside.

His kiss silenced her cry.

Fucking hell.

He gripped the edge of the desk and pounded into her, one hand on her hip.

"Jesus Liv. We are doing this every fucking meeting."

She half laughed as another orgasm built. One look at Fletcher and his expression matched the swelling of his cock inside her.

"I'm coming. Fuck, I'm coming inside you. In my goddamn office," he cried, his jaw clenched.

Best meeting ever.

CHAPTER TWENTY-NINE

Jesus, he'd never been so nervous for a date. This one was different, though. This morning he was taking two girls out.

Or at least a little girl and her sexy mom.

It had been his idea. One, because he wanted to see Olivia over the weekend while she had Sammy, *and* because he wanted to prove he wasn't concerned about her being a mom.

It was also so he could spend time with Sammy. If he and Olivia were going to be in a relationship, it was important he get to know Sammy and be introduced as her mom's boyfriend.

Or whatever Olivia wanted to refer to him as.

When he knocked, Sammy opened the door.

"Fletcher!" she said, jumping up and down.

"Hey squirt. Excited for our day out?"

"Yup. Ice cream, right? Mom said there would be ice-cream," she replied as Olivia appeared behind her, looking absolutely gorgeous.

He missed sleeping with her every night, but hopefully that would soon change.

"There will be ice-cream but first we have a little drive. Are you ready?" Fletcher asked.

"A drive? Where are we going this early on a Saturday?" Olivia laughed as Sammy nodded eagerly and reached to pick up her little pink backpack beside the door.

"Hop into the car and you'll see," he grinned, waving them down the stairs to where Frederick was parked.

They drove the ten miles to Wave Hill. Or, as it was often referred to, The Garden of Wonders.

It was twenty-eight acres of public gardens, woodlands and sprawling lawns perched above the Hudson River where a lot of families went to enjoy a day out. There were all sorts of activities, such as art for kids, nature walks and story time.

He'd thought it was something they could all enjoy.

"Oh, wow. I've always wanted to bring you here, Sammy," Olivia said, as they climbed out of the back seat of the car.

Fletcher mentally patted himself on the back and tugged his baseball cap down in the hope no one would recognize him. The last thing they wanted was media attention.

After they had wandered around for a few hours, Sammy chasing butterflies and squirrels, he led them over to the area where families were painting.

"Are you artistic?" Olivia asked.

"Absolutely not, but I figured Sammy would like it. How hard can it be to paint a tree or vase?" He shrugged.

Hard, as it turned out.

When Sammy began talking to some of the other kids and the staff member set them up, Olivia leaned into him and kissed him on the cheek. "Thank you. This is amazing."

He cupped her face and kissed her lips, sharing an intense gaze with her before Sammy caught them.

Fletcher was well aware that was taking it too far for the little girl.

In the end, Sammy's painting was about ten times better than their terrible efforts. They had spent much of it darting glances at each other and grinning like idiots, nodding when Sammy asked questions and pointed things out.

At the end of the day, they finished with the promised ice-creams and wandered back to the car.

Sammy fell asleep, her head on Olivia's lap, on the way home.

Fletcher pulled Olivia against his shoulder and felt a sense of contentment he never knew he'd been missing. When he dropped them off, he stood by the car door waving as Olivia carried her sleepy daughter inside. He didn't want to cross that line just yet by playing stepdad.

There would be time for that soon.

Tomorrow night he would have Olivia back in his arms, naked, and he'd be another step closer to gaining her trust.

If only he could fight the niggling feeling that kept running down his spine.

Something told him the guy hadn't given up.

Instead, Fletcher got the sense that Simon was biding his time.

CHAPTER THIRTY

Olivia ran down the hall and burst into Fletcher's office.

She knew he had an office full of people, including Daniel, and didn't give a shit.

She didn't care about anything right now except Sammy.

"Olivia?" Fletcher stood abruptly when he saw her and moved across the room to her.

"He's taken her!" she cried. "He's taken Sammy."

CHAPTER THIRTY-ONE

"So, you dropped her off at her father's house on Sunday night?" the NYC detective asked for the third time.

"Yes! For God's sakes. Now when are you going to look for her?" Olivia yelled.

Fletcher wanted to do the same thing. Instead, he was pacing.

"Who do I need to call?" he ground out. "The mayor? Who?"

One of the detectives gave him a look. "We know who you are, Mr. Dufort. You can call whoever you like but we still need to gather all the information from Ms. Miller before we send our teams out on what could be a wild goose chase."

He knew that, but sitting here feeling like he was doing nothing while the calm police detectives casually asked questions was hell.

No one knew where Sammy was, and Olivia kept staring at him, shaking, with tears falling down her face. He'd promised to protect them, and now her daughter was missing.

He needed to do something. Punch something.

"So, she's with her father?" The tall blond one asked.

"Yes, but he's... he's not..."

Fletcher knew this was a tough question to answer for Olivia. As far as officials knew, he was a world-class father.

Instead of a world-class asshole.

"She hasn't been in school for two days. They phoned me because they hadn't heard from her father, and I can't get hold of him. He always calls me back."

The detective wrote down the notes on his pad.

In the slowest handwriting in the universe.

For fuck's sake.

"What school does she go to?" he asked and ignored the look the cops gave him as she answered.

"If you could let us do our job, please, Mr. Dufort? Now what is your ex-husband's name?"

"Mantle. Simon Mantle."

"Okay, let's go through this again." Blond Cop spoke, and Fletcher rolled his eyes.

Jesus fucking Christ. They could make another child faster than this.

"Excuse me a moment," he said, and Olivia shot him a panicked look. He leaned down and kissed her. "I'll be back in a few minutes."

Fletcher closed the door behind him and walked to the car.

"Everything all right boss?" Frederick asked.

"Sammy's been taken," he answered. "I need to make a confidential call. Excuse me."

"Yes, sir," Frederick answered, and the privacy screen slid into place.

It was better nobody overhear this. He pressed dial.

"Adrian Black," a deep voice answered.

"Fletcher Dufort. I need your help."

An hour later, the detectives left.

He pulled Olivia into his arms, and she collapsed against his chest. "I feel so useless. Just staying here. Where the fuck is my little girl?"

"We're going to get her back, Liv. I promise." Fletcher lifted her face to his. "I've got a private investigative firm,"—or rather, a group of former marines, black ops dangerous mother fuckers, but details, details—"searching for her as well."

"You do?" she gasped.

He nodded. "Fuck yes. Money may not buy happiness, sweetheart, but it could just get Sammy back."

They sat down and went through everything she knew again, and then, when she finally fell into a fitful sleep in his arms, he rang Adrian Black again, relaying the further details.

"My team will get started on this immediately. We don't have any tolerance for people that hurt kids. You have our full commitment on this."

"Thank you. Let me know what I can do."

"Pay the deposit. I just sent you the invoice," Black said.

He let out a small laugh. "Yeah, no problem."

"Your next question is going to be how long. I don't know. But with the technology and the connections we have, I'm hoping to have Sammy Mantle back with her mother in forty-eight hours max."

"You can't promise that." He wasn't stupid.

"Unless she's no longer breathing, I can," Black said.

Jesus.

"How do you want us to deal with the father?"

Fucking hell. He didn't want this kind of decision weighing on his conscience. Right now he didn't want the guy breathing, but he wasn't ordering anyone's death.

"Evidence. He needs to lose all rights to his daughter at the very least, and I want him out of this city."

"You're a better man than me, Fletcher Dufort. I'd castrate the fucker," Black said darkly.

Well, that was still a possibility.

"If he's hurt her, I might just change my mind." He rubbed his forehead. Right now, he had to assume the man loved his daughter and this entire game was just to fuck with Olivia.

But he'd crossed the line. Enormously.

Fletcher wanted the man out of their lives. Out of Sammy's life. It wasn't his call to make, but Olivia would be insane if she let her daughter near her dad again. Once they had her back—because they *were* getting her back—he was going to speak to Liv about the fear that was crippling her from making important decisions.

It would be an uncomfortable conversation, but as someone who wasn't intimidated by the asshole, he could see how Simon had held her as an emotional prisoner for too long.

Olivia loved her daughter and wanted her to have a father, but there was a line. Simon was proving to be far too unstable for Sammy to be with.

Fletcher wanted them both safe.

End of story.

And that meant removing Simon from their lives.

"Trust me. If Mantle has hurt the child, he will never see his daughter or the Statue of Liberty ever again."

CHAPTER THIRTY-TWO

The next twenty-four hours were the longest of his life. Olivia paced the house, only sleeping for minutes at a time, and only when he forced her to lie down. He spent most of the time staring at his phone, waiting for it to ring.

Hunter, Daniel, and Harper had come over, offering support, and bringing food. Which still sat on the kitchen bench, getting cold.

No one could eat.

Harper's friend, Addison, had arrived at one point, and he immediately liked her. It could have been all the cursing and hate she flung towards Simon, but mostly because she seemed like a loyal and caring friend.

Olivia had cried in her arms as the two embraced on the sofa.

Olivia introduced Harper to her friend, and the two women appeared to get along well, under the somber circumstances.

"Do you have any idea where he would have taken her?" Addison asked.

Olivia shook her head.

"What about Emma? Have you tried to call her?"

Everyone was asking the same questions, but just as they all did, her friend wanted to help and needed answers herself.

"God, I feel so bad. Sienna said Sammy wasn't at school on Monday and I didn't suspect a thing," Addison said, shaking her head. "I should have."

"Don't. We couldn't have known. Kids get sick. You know that." Olivia wiped her eyes. "Fuck."

Fletcher watched painfully as Olivia went to all the dark places, worrying. He hated she was going through this. He hated that Sammy might be scared, hurt, or worse.

It was the 'worse' part that had them all frozen in fear. It was unthinkable and yet they had to mentally prepare for it to be a reality. Fletcher was planning to bring it up with her tonight after everyone left. Sammy had been gone three days now, even though they'd only learned about the disappearance yesterday.

It was a long time for a lot of things to happen.

He had no idea how she would react, but it was his job to support her through this.

"Do you think he'd hurt her? Like really hurt her?" Olivia asked, her voice trembling.

Well, fuck. Looked like they were talking about it now.

She looked up at him, and like a magnet, he pulled her to him as she threw herself into his chest. He wrapped his arms tightly around her.

As he looked over her shoulder, he saw Daniel full of fury, just as he imagined *he* must look right now. A quick glance at Hunter and he spotted his brother's clenched fists.

All three of them were protective men. Seeing someone hurt, knowing a child was in danger, was not fucking okay.

"Did you call Black?" Daniel asked under his breath.

"Yesterday."

"Good," he said firmly. "Let me know what I can do. Money. Whatever."

Fletcher shook his head and let out a short, dry laugh. "Stop offering me damn money. You know what my net worth is, dick."

Hunter snorted.

Olivia lifted her face. "Money for what?"

"Getting your daughter back. The private detectives." He shot Daniel a look that said leave it right there. His brother nodded in return.

Fletcher sat on the sofa and pulled Olivia to him, then glanced at Addison. She smiled at him and nodded.

Thank you, she mouthed, and he gave her a small smile.

"Fuck, I feel useless," Hunter spat out an hour later, standing and pacing. "Isn't there somewhere we could look? Or something?"

"Me too," Addison said, nodding knowingly at Hunter.

They all felt the same way.

Sitting around doing nothing was the most infuriating and disempowering feeling. Staying home, where the phone could ring, or Sammy could return, was the best advice the detectives had given them, and Fletcher knew they were right.

He could go looking, but Black Hawke had the expertise and technology to find her. By hiring the private company, he was giving them the best shot at finding Sammy.

Hopefully alive.

"Needle in a haystack. Like the cops said," Fletcher said.

"I need to punch something," Hunter said, sliding his phone into his back pocket. "Your ex-husband would be good, but a punching bag will do in the meantime."

Olivia gave him a sad smile. "Thanks Hunter."

"Call me if you need anything," he said, and Fletcher nodded.

"I'm going to head home, too. I'll be right back if you need me or pick up the phone if you want to talk," Addison said, and began tapping on her phone, obviously ordering an Uber.

"I'll give you a ride home," Hunter said.

Fletcher narrowed his eyes and Daniel shot him a look.

Interesting.

"Oh. You sure?" Addison blushed.

"Yeah. You can distract me, so I don't get road rage." He winked.

Oh boy.

Fletcher hoped this wasn't going in the direction he thought it was. Addison had no idea the type of sex life his brother enjoyed. He doubted very much it was the same as hers.

Or that of most people.

Daniel cleared his throat. "We should probably go, too. We can give you a ride, Addison," Daniel said, and Harper nodded beside him.

Addison looked between the two men while Hunter rolled his eyes at Daniel.

"I think I've got this, thanks bro. Come on, Addison, I don't bite and I'm much more fun than those two lovebirds." He placed a hand on Addison's back and led her out.

Fletcher nearly snorted.

He was pretty sure Hunter did bite, but at least Olivia was far too deep in shock to notice. She simply waved farewell to her friend.

Daniel looked at Fletcher and he shrugged.

Addison was a grown woman. Hunter wasn't going to pressure her into anything. He may be into darker things than either of them, but he didn't cross consent lines.

She could, and likely *would*, say no.

Right now, he had a more important problem to focus on.

Getting Sammy home.

CHAPTER THIRTY-THREE

Olivia lay on Fletcher's chest, staring into the darkness. Never in all the scenarios she'd imagined had she ever considered Simon might kidnap their daughter.

Was it kidnapping if he was her father?

In her mind it was.

The cops were searching for him, but they weren't treating it as an official kidnapping yet. Why not? His employer hadn't heard from him, and Emma, his wife, was also missing.

Had he snapped?

Were they alive?

She just didn't fucking know.

Fletcher was gently breathing, which meant he had finally fallen asleep. It had been thirty-seven hours—yes, she was counting every single one of them—since she'd run into his office. Between the two of them, they'd probably had about ten hours sleep.

Or even less.

They were both a mess.

She didn't know how she could have handled this without him. He had been her rock through this, and while it wasn't over and she had no idea how it was going to end, she was so grateful he was there.

She just couldn't imagine her life without Fletcher now. Him or Sammy.

She let out a little sob, pushing her face into the pillow so as not to wake Fletcher.

If only they could find her little girl and bring her home. Whoever *they* were.

She didn't care who the people were that Fletcher had hired, as long as they saved Sammy.

Then she had to find a way to keep Simon out of their lives once and for all. She didn't know how, but she was sick of being controlled.

And now he'd shown his true colors.

First, they had to find Sammy.

Fletcher's arms tightened around her as if knowing she needed the comfort even as he slept. She closed her eyes, leaning into him further.

Then, what felt like minutes, but in fact was about an hour later, Fletcher's phone rang.

He shot up and grabbed it like there was a bomb about to explode.

"Dufort," he answered, then cleared his voice from sleep.

She didn't know who they were, but a dark voice said very clearly, "We have her. Alive."

Olivia clasped her hand over her mouth and let out a guttural cry. Fletcher reached for her as he replied. "Where are you? What do we need to do?"

She scrambled out of bed and switched on the light, then dressed as he nodded, listening to the caller. His big eyes never left hers.

Then he hung up.

"Let's go."

CHAPTER THIRTY-FOUR

He was impressed Olivia hadn't asked him one single question. She had simply sat in the passenger seat, clenching her hands together and staring out into the dark of the early morning as he drove to the address Adrian Black had given him.

"You might have to wait in the car," he said.

"What?" Her head shot around. "Why? No. If they have Sammy—"

"Liv, I just don't know. These people are… we have to do as they ask, okay?" he replied.

She nodded, and he kept driving.

"But they have her?"

"Yes."

"'K."

And that was it. He pulled into the parking lot of a Lower Manhattan building and saw the white van.

"Oh, God." Olivia said, bursting into tears.

He reached for her hand and squeezed. He knew what she was thinking. It felt like they were in some fucking horror movie or serial killer documentary being reenacted.

"Stay here. Please," he said.

He might trust Black Hawke with recovering Sammy, but that was out of necessity. He wasn't putting Olivia anywhere near them. If he could have left her at home he would have, but there was no way she would stay there, and he would never ask that of her.

He pulled on his jacket and baseball cap and, shooting her one last look, he got out of the car.

As he approached the van two men got out. They were massive.

He was six foot two with a wide chest and shoulders, but these guys had height and a truck load of muscle on him.

Thank God he'd texted Daniel the details before he left. He wasn't *that* concerned, but he wasn't fucking stupid either.

"Dufort."

"Black?" he asked, and the man nodded, shaking his hand.

Almost crushing it.

"She's in the back, asleep. We sedated her to make it easier on her," Black said.

He nodded, shifting the cap on his head.

"Where did you find her?" Fletcher asked.

"Near Hudson Valley, just outside New York. Mantle's family has a cabin there. He had the child and wife roped up. Both were distraught. The woman is bruised and has broken ribs. As far as we can tell, Sammy is unharmed. Physically, at least, but you'll want to get her checked out."

Fletcher cursed.

Fucking asshole.

How was he going to tell Olivia this?

"We have photos that are on this drive, and the police are at the scene." Black handed him a flash drive. "They let us take Sammy. I pulled some big strings to make that happen."

"Thank you." Fletcher turned to the other man.

"This is Josh Hawke. My business partner," Black said.

An all-round terrifying looking guy. The kind you didn't fuck with.

The man reached out and they shook hands. "I helped Daniel with your senator friend."

"We're keeping you busy."

"And rich."

"Yeah." He let out a dry laugh, knowing it to be the truth, but both jobs had been invaluable. None more so than getting an innocent child returned to her mother.

Hawke crossed his muscular arms and shook his head. "Could have been worse, Dufort, but this fucker doesn't deserve to have a kid."

His stomach curled.

He wasn't sure he would ever look at the photos on the drive, or show Olivia. What would it help?

"As promised, we'll make sure Simon Mantle never gets near his daughter, or NYC, again. You can reassure her mother but when it's taken care of, I'll give you a call," Black said.

Hawke opened the side of the van and inside Fletcher saw Sammy's little body wrapped in blankets.

Jesus. His heart clenched, and he shook away the tears threatening to fill his eyes.

Black slapped him on his shoulder. "Tougher men than you have cried over the harm done to a child, my friend."

God damn him. He wiped his forearm across his eyes.

"Mother fucker," Fletcher mumbled.

"Yeah. He is," Black replied. "Offer still stands to upgrade your job."

Yeah, he knew what that meant, and he couldn't answer. Not right now.

Not as Hawke was handing Sammy to him. Fletcher took her from the man and pulled her against his chest, staring down into her innocent little face.

God. There wasn't anything he wouldn't do for her and her mother.

He made the decision right there and then.

They were both his.

Forever.

CHAPTER THIRTY-FIVE

The next morning, he sat at the table while Sammy was spoon fed her breakfast.

"Mommy, I can do it," she said, taking the spoon from Olivia.

He had slept on the sofa while Sammy and Olivia slept in her bed. He wasn't leaving them. Ever.

They just didn't know it yet.

Olivia had stayed in the car until he had walked back with Sammy in his arms and then she'd ripped open the door and leaped out, sobbing. Fletcher had put them both in the back seat, laying Sammy out so her head was on her mom's lap.

Then they had driven to the hospital.

After a handful of questions, the medical team had taken Sammy and Olivia and done the tests that needed to be done.

But it was important they knew.

And by early morning they did.

Simon hadn't touched her. Not in that way.

Thank fucking God.

She did, though, have bruises around her wrists, arms, and thighs, and was extremely upset, clinging to her mother.

But with time and support, she would heal.

Fletcher watched the two of them fighting over the spoon and continued making his plans. Biding his time.

Two weeks later, Sammy was back at school, and Fletcher had hired personal security for her.

Olivia hadn't tried to refuse him. He loved she was letting him help now. She trusted him and that made him happy.

It meant his plans were coming together.

The security woman, Frankie, drove Sammy to school and was positioned around the school grounds and classrooms, then took her home. Sammy thought it was fantastic. Her own special driver. She'd asked if Frankie could take her to get ice cream if she wanted and who was he to say no?

He hadn't needed to.

Olivia had.

Today, they were headed to a meeting. Or at least Olivia thought they were. Fletcher stood in the elevator as they made their way to the 103rd floor of the building in Manhattan.

"Fletcher, why are we meeting up here?" Olivia asked, sliding on her raspberry lip gloss.

"I don't know. This is where they wanted to meet. Possibly because of the photo opportunity." He shrugged, his hand clinging to the box in his pocket.

"Why didn't they send the details to me directly?" she asked, frowning.

"You can ask them yourself in a few minutes." He leaned in to kiss her.

Standing back, Fletcher slipped a finger inside his collar, tugging.

Was it hot?

Or was he freaking the fuck out?

Yeah, probably that the latter.

What if she said no?

God, he never thought he'd be doing this. And it was such a cliché place to do it, but they had Sammy full time and there was *no way* Olivia was letting her out of her sight for a night in the foreseeable future.

So, this was the best he had come up with.

They stepped out onto the secret VIP observation deck of the Empire State Building.

It was empty.

As he'd planned.

"Holy heck," Olivia said, walking to the edge. "It's magnificent up here. I didn't even know it existed."

When he didn't answer, she turned. "Did you?"

He was already down on one knee in front of her.

Please don't fucking say no.

"Oh my God!" she cried, her hand going to her chest.

"I told you I wouldn't do this in your living room, and I meant it." He grinned nervously and took a deep breath.

She stared at him with big open eyes.

"Olivia, I cannot sleep another night on the sofa." Fletcher smirked, as he took her hand.

He was lying. He'd totally sleep on it a million nights if that's what it took to be with her.

She grinned at his joke, as he'd hoped.

"So I've come up with a solution. You have to marry me."

Tears filled her eyes.

"Oh, and I forgot to mention one other little thing. I fucking love you. Beyond words. I never want to live a day without you or Sammy in my life. You are my everything. My heart, my soul, my love, and hopefully, you'll be my wife."

A tear fell down her cheek.

He stood.

"Olivia Miller, will you please marry me?" Fletcher's heart thudded inside his chest.

"Yes," she said, wiping away the tear. "Fletch, yes. I would be honored to be your wife."

Thank God!

He claimed her lips, and she flung her arms around him. Then when they parted, he finally got to slide the oval five-carat pink diamond onto her hand.

"It's beautiful," she exclaimed.

"Not nearly as beautiful as you." He lifted her hand to his lips.

"I love you, Fletcher Dufort."

"Finally," he said, grinning.

"You always knew."

He did.

He knew Olivia loved him by the way she smiled at him from across the room, the way her eyes held his as they made love, the way she now made him lunch when she packed one for Sammy.

"I love you, Mrs. Dufort." He grinned, picking her up and spinning them around.

"Holy shit." She laughed and tossed her head back.

CHAPTER THIRTY-SIX

Six weeks later

"Quickly decide, Sammy. The movers can't stand around all day," Olivia said.

They could.

He was paying them, and if they needed to stay exactly where they were for the next eight hours while that gorgeous little girl of his decided on her bedroom, he'd fucking make them.

Fletcher would do anything for her.

Sammy had slid inside his heart and, like her mom, he'd decided she was his. Respectfully. He'd obviously need Olivia's permission, but he wanted to adopt her.

Once he had Liv's permission, he'd ask Sammy.

It was up to her if she wanted him to be her legal father, and that would take time.

For now, he was happy, knowing both of them were his to protect and love every single day.

"That one," Sammy said. "Is that okay, Fletch?"

"Whatever one you want, baby girl." He gave the movers a nod.

"Okay, that one." She nodded rapidly. "And can it be pink? No, purple. And pink."

Olivia laughed.

"Sorry about the change in décor," she said, leaning into him as he put his arm around her. "You might not be winning any more awards now we're living with you."

He dropped his lips to hers. "I won *all* the awards the moment you said yes to marrying me."

Sammy giggled and snuck between them for a cuddle. Fletcher picked her up, and Olivia kissed her on the cheek.

"I'm going to be the flower girl, right?" she asked, and they both nodded.

Again.

It was as if his entire body relaxed the moment their belongings moved into his—their—home. Where they belonged.

Later that night, when Sammy was tucked up in her new bedroom, Fletcher and Olivia curled up on the sofa with some mindless TV show playing in the background.

"Happy?" he asked.

"Yes. You?"

"Very," he said. "I heard from my contact earlier today. Simon was sentenced to twenty-two years in prison."

Fletcher had waited until they were alone to tell her. It was an emotional time, waiting to find out what his term would be. They knew he wouldn't be let free but it had been unclear for how long.

"Thank God," Olivia said. "It's not forever, but it's something."

"He won't ever have custody of Sammy again, so that's the important thing. But there's something else," he said, and her eyes widened. "Your name has been cleared. The drug charges are gone."

Her mouth fell open. "How?"

Fletcher shook his head. "We don't ask questions; we just say thank you."

Olivia nodded. "Thank you."

"Not to me. Them."

"No," she said, taking his face in her hands. "You. You did all of this for me. I know its cost you far more than I could ever repay."

He frowned and lifted her onto his lap.

"Baby, all that I have is yours now. Every cent I have. I'd spend it all, if I had to, to have you and Sammy in my life. Best investment ever."

Olivia shook her head in a show of disbelief, and he smiled lovingly at her. He planned to prove it to her every day.

"I love you, Fletcher Dufort."

"Music to my ears, nearly wife." His eyes darkened, and her breath caught.

He slowly undid the buttons on her top and slid her lacy bra down so he could place his mouth over her nipple. "Let me show you how much I love you."

He flipped her onto her back and pulled off her jeans. Once his own clothes were off, he lay over her and slid two fingers inside her, loving the gasp she released.

"I swear you are always wet for me."

"Always," she said, arching into him.

He circled his fingers, their mouths connecting and tongues dancing as he captured hers.

"Fuck me, Fletcher," she begged.

As his cock slowly pressed inside her, he stilled.

"What?" She smirked cheekily, as if she knew he had finally worked it out.

"You haven't…"

Her period.

Olivia shook her head.

Holy shit.

"Are you—" he asked, and she nodded and let out a little laugh.

Oh, my God.

Oh my God!

He slammed into her and rode them to pleasure as he held the eyes of the woman he loved. The woman who was going to be his wife *and* have his baby.

"It better be a boy or I'm going to go crazy protecting all my girls." He grinned afterwards. "By the way, how do you feel about me adopting Sammy?"

Olivia nodded in his arms, both of them naked, sprawled on the sofa. "I had a feeling you might ask."

He lifted his head, waiting for her answer

"The answer is yes. If Sammy agrees," she said and, in that moment, Fletcher felt like his life was complete.

He couldn't wait to make Olivia his wife, meet their child, and make Sammy his.

Loving the Dufort Dynasty series?

Read Hunter and Addison's steamy dark billionaire romance, Total Possession, next.
Turn the page or buy your eBook or paperback at one of the links below:

www.juliettebanks.com
books2read.com/ForbiddenTouch-Dufort

If you love steamy romances with a paranormal twist, download <u>The Vampire Prince</u> **for FREE** and meet my bestselling Moretti Blood Brother vampires.

ALSO BY JULIETTE N. BANKS

Visit **www.juliettebanks.com** to check out the rest of my steamy romances.

The Dufort Dynasty
Steamy billionaire romance
Sinful Duty
Forbidden Touch
Total Possession

The Moretti Blood Brothers
Steamy paranormal romance
The Vampire Prince **FREE**
The Vampire Protector
The Vampire Spy
The Vampire's Christmas
The Vampire Assassin
The Vampire Awoken
The Vampire Lover
The Vampire Wolf
The Vampire Warrior

Read The Vampire King (FREE series starter)

Read The Vampire Origin (FREE short story)

TOTAL
POSSESSION

CHAPTER ONE

Hunter stepped into the elevator and tugged on the sleeves of his black Prada blazer.

He was late.

On purpose.

Which was an asshole thing to do, given it was his brother Fletcher's engagement party.

He wished they'd all stop getting engaged. By *they*, he meant his two brothers. Both had. Which left him as the sole Dufort bachelor.

And didn't the New York media know it, and regularly mention it.

He hated the spotlight being on him and had been relying on Fletcher to remain single and uphold his title as the Playboy of Manhattan.

Then he'd gotten all hot and heavy with his PR manager and was now engaged, a stepfather to Olivia's daughter, Sammy, and expecting a child.

Their older brother, Daniel, was getting married to his Kiwi girlfriend, Harper.

How in the holy fuck did that all happen?

The brothers had all sworn off marriage in their late teenage years after watching their philandering father destroy their mother.

Well, he wasn't going to lose his mind like those two airheads.

The likelihood of that happening was very low given his tastes.

And he wasn't talking about whiskey.

Which he very much liked.

His bedroom tastes, if one could call it that given he rarely made it to a bed when fucking women, was darker than that of most people.

He wasn't a sadist.

He just needed to be in control.

Complete control.

His style wasn't for everyone.

Nor were the women who enjoyed being submissive to a dominant lover the type, generally, to be looking for marriage.

Although those who learned his surname quickly changed their mind.

Dufort.

He was a billionaire.

So were his two brothers.

As equal majority shareholders of the Dufort Dynasty, a legacy that included the global Dufort Hotel group, the three brothers were all the penultimate bachelors.

Or had been.

With good looks and charm on their side, along with their bank balances, thanks to their father Johnathan Dufort, who had created the company, women wanted to marry them, and men wanted to be them.

Or fuck them over.

It was the cold hard truth they had all learned very quickly.

So, no, Hunter wasn't concerned about falling into matrimonial bliss. And that wasn't why he had purposely delayed attending Fletcher and Olivia's engagement party this evening.

The elevator doors opened.

He was immediately greeted with the smells and scents of a cocktail party, along with Fletcher's multi-million-dollar view.

"Good evening, sir." A roaming waiter with a tray of champagne greeted him.

"Evening. I'll have a whiskey please. On the rocks," Hunter replied.

"Yes, sir."

He didn't bother smiling as he made his way through the crowd. Everyone knew he was the brooding type, so why prove them wrong?

He hated large groups, much preferring one-on-one time with people, or smaller social events.

This was just the tip of the iceberg. There were two big weddings to follow these damn engagement parties. Daniel's would be in the middle of summer which was only a month away.

"Nice of you to finally arrive, dickhead," Fletcher said as he joined his brothers in the living room.

The waiter arrived with his whiskey.

"Cheers. Happy engagement and all that." He ignored his brother and gave Olivia a grin.

Broody he may be, but he had all the Dufort charm and knew his hazel eyes and dimples worked their magic.

"Thank you, Hunter," Olivia said and accepted his kiss on the cheek.

They weren't strangers. Olivia had worked for their company for over two years now and as the director of sales, he worked closely with Fletcher and his marketing team.

"Welcome to the family," he added.

"Right where she belongs," Fletcher said, wrapping his arm around Olivia's back, and kissing her forehead.

The two stared into each other's eyes like total idiots so Hunter turned away and surveyed the crowd for the woman he was avoiding.

Because he was avoiding her, very much.

It had been a month since he last saw her.

Since he met her one night at Olivia's when her daughter Sammy had been kidnapped by her ex-husband.

It was the most inappropriate time to meet a woman and want to fuck her into complete submission.

But that was what had happened.

Not that Hunter had fucked her.

And likely never would.

He suspected Addison Hill was as vanilla as they came. Someone needed to tell his cock that.

Hunter had dropped her off home that night and it had been awkward. She was clearly overwhelmed by his wealth and being so close to him. He'd lost count of how many times she'd blushed and looked away from him.

Yet, he'd had an erection the entire drive home and if he hadn't had a t-shirt on covering his damn jeans, she would have seen it.

Although he doubted she had the courage to look at his groin without dying of embarrassment.

He'd made small talk with her, casting looks down at her, as he worked his way through the New York traffic, and she'd chatted easily enough.

Addison was gorgeous, there was no doubting that. Her short wavy blond hair looked more suited to California than New York, but he could tell she was a stylish woman. She wore a pair of distressed jeans, a white crop top and long dark cardigan, with boots.

That hint of skin above her jeans had been fucking with his head since he walked in the door of Olivia's house.

While he wasn't completely disengaged from the trauma of finding the missing child—because the situation had totally infuriated him—his eyes kept drifting to Addison.

Given the opportunity he'd unzip those jeans, rip up her top and suck on those breasts while fucking her with his fingers.

Then he'd make her wait.

And the games would begin.

She'd caught him looking and he'd snuck her a slow dirty smirk. Her blush had given him pause. She could be the perfect submissive, but something told him she wasn't.

He probably could have left it there, but when he pulled up at her building Addison had turned to him from the front seat of his Aston Martin and lowered her eyes.

Fuck, his cock had fought to get out of his jeans.

She'd tugged her bottom lip between her teeth and those eyes of hers had slowly lifted and locked on his, looking for instruction.

He'd taken her chin in his hand. "Be careful what you ask for, Addison."

Her lips had parted and he couldn't look away from the glistening invitation inside.

"I will take everything you have to give if you want to play. If not, I recommend you hop out of the vehicle now."

As Hunter watched her mind swirl, trying to calculate the risk versus pleasure—if she even knew what he was offering—the clock ticked.

He began to think she was going to nod.

Her eyes had dropped to his crotch.

He'd smirked.

"You want to try before you buy?" he asked, raising an amused brow.

Then her gaze had shot to his, and he'd known. She had too much fire in her. She would be fun to break, but she was Olivia's friend. It was too close to home.

He dropped her chin and leaned back in his seat.

"Goodnight, Addison."

"Wha—"

"Goodnight, Addison," he repeated. "Trust me. This is for the best."

The dark look she had given him only confirmed he'd made the right decision.

Except those lips, that skin, and her sexy ass as she'd run into her building had haunted him.

Now, tonight, he would see her again.

And he wasn't sure he could say no a second time.

LOVING THE SERIES?

Read Hunter and Addison's
steamy dark billionaire romance,
Total Possession, next.

Buy your eBook or paperback at one of the
links below:

www.juliettebanks.com
books2read.com/TotalPossession

ALSO BY JULIETTE N. BANKS

To buy go to **www.juliettebanks.com** or any
online book retailer

The Dufort Dynasty
Steamy billionaire romance

The Moretti Blood Brothers
Steamy paranormal romance

LET'S STAY IN TOUCH

Join my BOOKCLUB
bit.ly/JNB_VIP_BOOKCLUB

READERS FACEBOOK GROUP
facebook.com/groups/authorjuliettebanksreaders

INSTAGRAM:
juliettebanksauthor

BOOKBUB:
Juliette N Banks

GOODREADS
goodreads.com/juliettenbanks